What Others Say about
Deep into Yellowstone

———

Eminent naturalist and wildlife advocate Rick Lamplugh draws from a deep personal wellspring of experience and knowledge to take readers into Yellowstone National Park's wild heart. In this superb weave of memoir, natural history, and public policy grounded in science, he shares life lessons from animals who have crossed his path and unflinching insights about what it will take to conserve bison, wolves, and grizzlies. The humility, honesty, and wisdom of these essays will resonate deeply for all readers.

Cristina Eisenberg, PhD, Chief Scientist, Earthwatch Institute, author

In this deeply personal accounting of a year in Yellowstone, Rick captures the experience of living at Yellowstone's doorstep—with all the joy and heartache that entails. An insightful journey through the seasons and natural history of Yellowstone, this book stands as a loving tribute to the park and all its complexities.

Jenny Golding, writer, and editor of AYellowstoneLife.com

With a touch of Bill Bryson's whimsy, a dose of Edward Abbey's insight, and the story-telling charm of John McPhee, *Deep into Yellowstone* is a sincere and intensely personal diary of shared adventures and observations. This page-turner is rich in humor and insight. I found it difficult to put down.

John Gillespie, geologist and Yellowstone instructor

Deep into Yellowstone is an engaging and very important book that deserves to be read by everyone who cares about wildlife and wildlands. Lamplugh's stories are filled with passion and heartache as he shares his love of Yellowstone and his search for how he—and we—can protect this land. His writings illuminate the intricate web that connects Yellowstone's plants and animals, and the habitat they depend on, as well as how the integrity of that web depends on humans making choices that will protect and cherish them in perpetuity.

Barbara J. Moritsch, author, *The Soul of Yosemite: Finding, Defending, and Saving the Valley's Sacred Wild Nature*

Rick Lamplugh is a word artist, and Yellowstone is his palette. Rick's words take me into Yellowstone...I hike with him on Blacktail Plateau, ski with him in Lamar Valley, wander the Upper Geyser Basin with him. From geology to bison to moose to wolves, Rick enthralls as he educates. Read *Deep into Yellowstone*, travel via words to this Wonderland, and come away with passion for and knowledge of the heated controversies surrounding our first national park.

Julianne Baker, Yellowstone instructor and blogger at *Writing the Wild*

Travel through the chapters along with Rick, as he gives you an upfront view to some of Yellowstone National Park's most controversial issues. Sharing truthful perspectives that are downright heartbreaking and occasionally comical, Rick gives you a powerful, observant, and caring look into our world's first National Park. Reinforced by copious facts, this book is a great read by a local author. By reading these pages, you too might find your inner 'meanderthal'…

MacNeil Lyons, owner, Yellowstone Insight

Who has not wished for a year away from urbanization to immerse oneself into nature and the world surrounding it? Rick made that immersion happen. He engaged nature one-on-one from his new home in Gardiner, Montana. He chronicled his year of fascination, reverence, and insight into nature and society encompassing one of the last remnants of the natural world, Yellowstone National Park. With Rick as a mentor and guide share his veneration and fear for the future of Yellowstone while you contemplate your role in the future of the planet.

Jim Halfpenny, PhD, Pres., A Naturalist's World

Uprooting his whole life, Lamplugh moves to Yellowstone to go "all in" on the park experience. Deeply immersed in the primitive landscape, he portrays his explorations and transformative wildlife encounters with skillful intimacy. These are more than pretty words—a grim reality threatens Yellowstone's iconic species, the bison, the wolf, and the grizzly bear.

Nathan Varley, PhD, co-owner, Yellowstone Wolf Tracker

Through rich storytelling and engaging prose, *Deep Into Yellowstone* illuminates the struggles today's Yellowstone faces. As a decade-long resident and wildlife biologist in the park, I was both entertained and informed. Whatever your relationship to Yellowstone, this book will make that relationship more meaningful.

Lisa Baril, science and nature writer

Deep into Yellowstone explores complex issues facing America's first national park. Lamplugh takes the reader along a journey of getting to know the wild places and issues that face Yellowstone. Like many, Rick and his wife Mary visited Yellowstone and fell in love. They join their neighbors and lend their voices for the sake of the wildlife and wild lands they grew to love. This is not your typical ecological narrative; it's a human narrative. Readers can enjoy the scenery while learning about wolves, bison, climate change, gold mining on Yellowstone's doorstep, and more.

Michelle Uberuaga Z., Executive Director, Park County Environmental Council, environmental attorney

Deep into Yellowstone is a fine-tuned blend of the glories of the natural world and the ceaseless parade of battles we must fight to preserve these marvels. While we are entertained and awed by Lamplugh's rich portrayal of Yellowstone, he never fails to reveal the truth behind the beauty; the brutal history of the wolves, bison, antelope and other creatures, as well as the dismal fate that befalls them today. Yet, *Deep into Yellowstone* gifts us with hope and plenty of reason to advocate for the sanctity of Yellowstone and the environment everywhere.

Beckie Elgin, author, *Journey: The Amazing Story of OR-7, the Oregon Wolf that Made History*

Also by Rick Lamplugh

In the Temple of Wolves: A Winter's Immersion in Wild Yellowstone

Deep into Yellowstone

A Year's Immersion in
Grandeur and Controversy

Rick Lamplugh

Catalog information:
Deep into Yellowstone: A Year's Immersion in Grandeur and
Controversy / Rick Lamplugh. —1st edition.
1. Yellowstone National Park—Description and travel.
2. Ecology—Yellowstone National Park.
3. Natural History—Yellowstone National Park
4. Lamplugh, Rick—Journeys
5. Lamplugh, Rick, 1948-

ISBN: 1546448322
ISBN 13: 9781546448327

Printed in the United States of America on library-quality stock
10 9 8 7 6 5 4 3 2 1

For Mary, Allison, Zack, Hana, and Siena

Table of Contents

———

Winter

1

Wild Wolves in Action

———

As Mary and I drive toward home, tired and happy from a day of cross-country skiing, we enjoy the warm touch of low, western sun streaming through our car windows. The view beyond those windows is grand, northeastern Yellowstone at its best. The two-lane, snow-covered road snakes along the side of a narrow canyon cut by Soda Butte Creek. Two mountains crowd either side, both over 10,000 feet high, one draped with an abundance of frozen waterfalls.

Gradually, the canyon widens and we slow and scan for moose as we pass by Round Prairie. Moments later the sulfur scent of Soda Butte Cone—an ancient thermal feature— floats to us on the air from the car's heat vents. Further on, we pass a ridge where Bighorn sheep rest in the sun.

Rounding a curve, we enter our favorite part of Yellowstone National Park, the Lamar Valley. We lived in the heart of this wildlife-filled valley for three winters when we volunteered at the Lamar Buffalo Ranch. Those wild winters changed our lives, led us to leave Corvallis, Oregon, our home for thirty-five years, where we had raised our kids and crafted our careers. We moved to Gardiner, Montana, right next door to Yellowstone.

As we near the entrance road to the Buffalo Ranch, we see a swarm of cars crammed into a pullout.

"What do we have here?" Mary asks as she slows the car.

"I wonder if the Mollie's are here again today," I reply. The Mollie's, one of Yellowstone's wolf packs, lives most of the year in another valley south of here. But they swagger into the Lamar Valley each winter in search of prey. We heard yesterday that they have arrived.

After a day of skiing in silent splendor, neither of us is keen on being engulfed by a crowd, but the possibility of seeing those beautiful wolves in their healthy pack lures us in. Mary maneuvers into the last available spot and cuts the engine.

Outside we hear the excited chatter of some of the many visitors here for January's long Martin Luther King Jr. weekend. Some peer into spotting scopes trained on the base of Specimen Ridge, more than a mile away, across the valley floor. Located between us and the ridge, the Lamar River hides under ice and snow. A few of the Lamar Valley's often-photographed cottonwoods reveal its frozen, winding path.

"Hmm, let's see what's happening," Mary says. She reaches into the glove box for binoculars, brings them to her eyes, and focuses. Mary's vision is much better than mine; she has what I call guide eyes. I sit and wait for her to learn why everyone is here so late in the day.

"Holy smokes! It is the Mollie's!" she exclaims, amazement in her voice.

Thrilled, I gauge the general direction of her discovery, grab my camera and, using the telephoto lens like binoculars, zoom in on the pack, mostly black wolves and a few grays. They crouch, tails down, one behind the other, forming a long line that points west. I pan in the direction they stare and soon a group of about twenty bison, big adults, mid-sized yearlings, and smaller calves, fills my viewfinder. "Whoa! We're going to see them hunt bison!"

I can't believe our luck. The Mollie's are the only Yellowstone wolves that regularly take down adult bison. And we've never seen them do so. Few people have.

Mary tosses the binos onto the dashboard, jumps out of the car, and reaches into the backseat to grab her spotting scope.

As she hustles to the edge of the knee-high snow berm that lines the pullout and the road, I step out to watch the pack through the viewfinder. They start moving: first in a walk, then a trot, then a lope. "They're running!" I shout to Mary. As I swing the camera to the west, I say in a softer voice, "And so are the bison!"

"Oh, I'll never get this thing set up in time," Mary mutters, wrestling with the legs of the tripod.

"Take your time," I tell her. "This could last a while."

Once the tripod is stable, she'll attach her iPhone to the spotting scope, which will then function as a telephoto lens to pull the action in closer than I can with my handheld camera. I assume she'll video; I know I will. By studying our footage, we'll learn more about how wolves and bison interact in this rarely seen confrontation. We'll share the footage with friends—some are Yellowstone guides and instructors—and hear what they have to say. The chance to observe and learn like this is one of the reasons we moved here.

In the viewfinder, I follow the chase: the bison, running, tails up, bodies rocking up and down with their stiff-legged gait; the wolves, tails straight out, bodies arching and flowing as their legs fully extend to the front and rear. Then one of the winter-naked cottonwoods comes between me and the wolves, blocking my view. Damn! I grunt and yank the camera from my eye.

These wolves that fascinate us, these Mollie's, once called the Lamar Valley home. The pack—one of the first released during the controversial wolf reintroduction in 1995—was then named the Crystal Creek pack. While they denned near this location in the spring of 1996, the just-released Druid Peak pack attacked and killed the Crystal Creek's alpha male and every pup. The two surviving Crystal Creek wolves, the alpha female and a male, fled to Pelican Valley, about twenty miles south. The two denned the next year and produced a litter of six pups. Their pack grew and in 2000 was renamed to honor Mollie Beattie, the late director of the US Fish & Wildlife Service, who had been instrumental in returning wolves to Yellowstone. This year the pack contains sixteen wolves; six more than the average for park packs.

I look farther west and spot a place where I think I can video without being blocked by cottonwoods. I glance over at Mary; she has the scope set up and wears a frown of concentration as she wiggles the iPhone onto the eyepiece. Not wanting to disturb her, I leave the pullout without a word.

I walk by parked cars, past other excited watchers standing at silent scopes and clicking cameras, and onto the edge of the road. In the distance, the wolves and bison are still running. And now, so am I.

A few hundred yards later I step off the road and sink to my knees into the snow berm. The snow chills through my socks, and I realize that I am in low-cut shoes. In my rush to action, I neglected to put on the insulated boots that sit warm and dry in the car. I look back at the car, down at my snow-covered feet, and out at the wolves. No question: Wild wolves take precedence over warm feet. I raise the camera back to my eye. The Mollie's have sprinted past the bison they first chased and are near another group of about twenty adults, yearlings, and calves. The viewfinder scene rises and falls with my breathing, ragged after jogging at 6,600 feet of elevation. I chant aloud to myself, "Slow down. Breathe. Relax." I stabilize and so does the image. I push the RECORD button and settle into the thrill of capturing this spectacle.

The bison have raised their tails. That tail—short with long strands of fur at the tip—is a flag that denotes danger. The higher that flag, the more agitated the bison. As the old saying goes: a raised tail means charge or discharge. Now most of those tails are straight up, as high as they can go. I'm thinking charge.

The bison start to run en masse. As they gallop in an elongated cluster through snow that almost brushes their underbellies, their hooves kick up a low white fog that hangs in the air behind them. Some of the Mollie's run just behind the group, disappearing and reappearing in the fog. Other wolves lope beside the group, which has no stragglers and little space between the animals. If a careless wolf breached that group, it could be kicked, trampled, or gored. But the Mollie's know what they're doing. These experienced hunters are sorting and sifting, looking and listening and smelling for anything out of the ordinary, any sign that reveals a vulnerable bison, a possible meal.

Bison are part of, but not all of, this pack's diet. Their menu varies, depending on the time of year and location of their prey. From June through early November when elk roam the Mollie's Pelican Valley home, up to 80 percent of the pack's diet is elk. Once winter arrives and elk leave Pelican Valley, the pack has two options, according to a Yellowstone Wolf Project annual report. (The Wolf Project brought the wolves to Yellowstone from Canada and continues to study them.)

Their first option is to follow the elk. That's why the Mollie's return to the elk-heavy Lamar Valley each winter. They stay longer some years as opposed to others. One year, when they were the largest pack in Yellowstone, they lingered here for much of winter and spring.

Their second option is to stay in Pelican Valley and switch to eating bison. Bringing down a bison—an animal ten to fifteen times heavier than a wolf and armed with sharp horns and deadly hooves—is more dangerous than bringing down an elk and may take days. To improve their odds of success, the pack, as they are doing now, seeks vulnerability. Bison are most vulnerable during winter, and from January through April, bison make up at least 80 percent of the Mollie's diet.

When the Mollie's hunt bison during the winter in Pelican Valley, the area is not accessible by car. That's why so few people have witnessed these wolves take a bison. Could we be lucky enough to see them bring down one today in the Lamar Valley?

The chase continues away from where I stand and dwindles in my viewfinder. I trudge through deep snow back to the road. Once there, I trot in the direction the animals are running. There are no cars moving in either lane, but four cars, flashers blinking, windows down, and optics protruding have turned one lane of this public road into an illegal parking lot. I jog past the stationary vehicles and keep running until I'm out of breath. Luckily, I have reached a spot with an unobstructed view. I step off the road, look into the camera, again slow my breathing, and start recording.

Behind me, I hear tires crunch to a stop on the snow-covered road. Then Mary's excited voice: "Oh, there you are. I wondered where you'd gone." She chuckles. "Is this incredible or what?"

"I can't believe we're seeing this," I say, my eye still at the viewfinder.

"What are you going to do?" she asks.

"I'm going to stay here for a while and video. Why don't you go on to the next pullout?"

As Mary drives away, I smile, pleased by our shared focus on catching every possible moment of this wild action.

The bison stop running and tighten their formation. Their collective breath creates a cloud above their massive backs. The closest wolves stop too, awaiting other pack members. As the wolves arrive, they greet each other with a lick or a bump.

As hunters and hunted catch their breath, I look down the road for *my* packmate. Mary's probably at that next pullout, about three-quarters of a mile away. Joining her would put me closer to this scene and provide a better viewing angle. I start jogging again, passing more vehicles idling in the road. At the head of another illegal line, a man and woman have climbed out of their truck. She is setting up a spotting scope in the middle of the lane between her truck and the car parked behind it. I slow to a walk and duck my head as I pass in front of her scope.

When I glance again at the wolves, I see they have now encircled the group of bison; the next act in nature's play is about to begin. I pick up my pace and my panting. As I close in on the packed pullout, I spot our car but not Mary. I'm not surprised that she has sought a private place away from the crowd. Now I just have to find her. I jog past the pullout and there she is in her perfect spot: alone, well off the road, hunched over her scope in snow almost to her knees.

When I reach her, she flashes that smile I love: the I'm-so-excited-I-can-hardly-stand-it one. While Mary has a wonderful smile any time of year, this rendition usually appears only in Yellowstone. Then she points to her iPhone, signals me to silence, and returns to videoing. I move a few feet away, tramp a circle in the snow, squat, and rest my left elbow on my left knee to steady the camera. I put eye to the viewfinder and focus on the unfolding drama.

The bison have crowded together, big heads and sharp horns pointing outward, forming a prickly perimeter. The wolves stand nearby, panting and peering at the bison and one another. The standoff continues until a large female bison steps away from her group and toward four wolves. Three wolves immediately back away, but one stands its ground. The bison approaches until predator and prey are inches apart, noses nearly touching. Is she testing the wolves in the same way the wolves are testing the bison? The two stand statue-still, eyes locked. Who will blink first?

The wolf's mouth opens and closes, and a moment later the tough predator tucks its tail and backs away. With no hesitation, the bison takes four steps forward, head down, horns at the ready. Then, as if on cue, she and the wolf stop. The testing is over; neither animal will waste any more of the energy that's in such scant supply during winter.

Meanwhile, at the other end of the group, six black wolves and two grays have separated and surrounded another big female bison. She wears a leather collar that has a small white box attached to it. The box contains electronics that transmit data park biologists use to determine where bison roam.

But right now that white box broadcasts her mood to the wolves as it moves up and down with the aggressive bobbing of her head. The bison charges a gray wolf and then the half-ton ballerina spins to face two oncoming blacks. High-pitched wolf howls drift in from the east, a surreal soundtrack to this deadly dance.

"Oh my God," Mary whispers in awe. "This could be it."

I don't reply; I'm too engrossed watching the collared bison spin this way and that, keeping the wolves at bay. Yet despite all this dancing, I don't see the wolves biting, the bison goring or kicking.

The rest of the bison come to the collared female's aid. They surround her, snorting clouds of breath and kicking sprays of snow at the wolves. The hunters retreat to a safe distance. This is another way in which hunting bison is more dangerous than hunting elk. In an elk herd chased by wolves, it's every animal for itself. Not so with bison; these animals protect their own.

The bison continue lunging at the wolves. Finally, one by one, the wolves back off. Heads down, following in each other's steps, the predators climb a nearby slope. All that is except one, which has yet to disengage. The holdout walks through the group until a bison charges and chases. Then the lone wolf scoots for the safety of the pack. The bison, tails now down, watch the pack retreat.

At the top of the snow-covered rise, the Mollie's stop in a long, beautiful line, heads up, ears alert. They appear to be awaiting an order. Then the pack moves single file down the far side of the hill and out of our sight.

Mary and I step away from the optics, grin at each other and tap gloved knuckles. As we pack our gear and head for the car, we don't know whether the Mollie's have given up or whether their reconnaissance was productive and they will return with darkness, hungry and ready for the hard work of making dinner.

What we do know is that we were afforded a rare gift to have watched these wild wolves in action.

2

Making the Move

A few years ago, Mary and I spent our first January, February, and March living and working at the Lamar Buffalo Ranch in the heart of Yellowstone's wolf country. As volunteers, we drove a fourteen-passenger bus filled with excited seminar participants and their instructor over snowy roads. We helped our passengers spot wildlife. When not out driving, we worked at the ranch, shoveling snow and cleaning cabins. We observed wolves—including the Mollie's—almost every day. When not working or watching wolves, I journaled about our day-to-day life in the valley. By the time that first winter ended, we couldn't wait to volunteer the next winter.

When we left the Lamar Valley at the end of March, snow still covered the ground. When we arrived home in Corvallis a couple days later, the sights and scents of spring blooming were everywhere. But so were buildings, cars, and people. We commented to one another on how busy and noisy our "little" town of 55,000, half of them Oregon State University students, had become.

We convinced each other that any place would seem loud and crowded after spending three months in a wild valley with the closest neighbor eleven miles away. Of course, we had groups of seminar participants who would stay at the ranch for a few days. But after a group left, the six of us who lived at the ranch all winter often had a day or two when silence reigned. When bison scratched their backs on the sides of our log cabins. When wolves sauntered down the sidewalk. When coyotes sang. How, we asked, could any place compare to that? Oh, come on, we answered, let's just settle back into our Corvallis life and see what happens.

What happened was that Mary became part of a ukelele trio. She enjoyed the hours of practice and rehearsal that built to each exciting performance. While she played music, I reviewed those journal entries from the first winter and started writing *In the Temple of Wolves: A Winter's Immersion in Wild Yellowstone*. As we pursued our interests, the familiarity and routine of Corvallis lulled us back into a feeling of normalcy.

At the end of December, we packed our minivan, drove 1,000 miles over five snowy mountain passes, and arrived at the ranch. That second winter, sadly, was much quieter than the first. The valley did not resound with the howls of the Lamar Canyon pack. We did not see those familiar wolves resting on the hillside above the ranch. Instead, we felt the shock and sadness of watching the pack disintegrate.

Just weeks before we arrived, the pack's famous alpha female, nicknamed 06 (oh-six) by admiring wolf watchers, had been shot outside the park in the shoot-a-wolf-anytime-anywhere-for-any-reason rampage that Wyoming officials had the nerve to call a wolf hunt. With 06 gone, the alpha male needed a new mate. One dawn we watched him howl goodbye to his pack and walk west, leaving the Lamar Valley in search of another female. Part of his pack stayed east of the park where their mother had been killed. The rest passed through the Lamar Valley on occasion, but none stayed.

That one gunshot by a trophy hunter had essentially killed the whole Lamar Canyon pack. Observing firsthand the destructive impact of hunting on those wolves we had come to know and respect, started me thinking about advocating for the protection of wolves.

Though there were fewer wolves to watch that second winter, we stayed busy with driving, cleaning, and shoveling. In my time off, I dug into researching the book-in-progress. I observed with all my senses; listened to and talked with experts that came to teach seminars; and dug into the hundreds of books, videos, and maps that lined the shelves of the ranch library. The more I learned about the social behavior and positive impact of wolves on the ecology of the Lamar Valley, the more I came to admire these essential predators.

When we returned to Oregon after the second season, we sensed that the town we had called home for more than three decades would never be the same. Corvallis seemed even noisier and more crowded than just a year before. Mary and I had our first discussion about whether we should move. And, if so, where? To some rural spot outside of town? To the Oregon coast? To Gardiner, Montana?

We laughed the first time one of us mentioned moving to Gardiner, a town with about 850 year-round residents and situated right on Yellowstone's northern border. As a Yellowstone gateway, Gardiner lives or dies on the money tourists leave behind. Much of the town is shut down from October to May when visitors are scarce. The regional shopping area and hospital are in Livingston, fifty-two miles away via a high-speed, two-lane highway. So many elk, bison, mule deer, big horn sheep, and pronghorn are struck by vehicles on that stretch of road that locals call it "The Gauntlet."

When we lived at the Buffalo Ranch, we saw Gardiner as a tiny, rundown, high-desert town with more wind and less snow than the Lamar Valley. Only necessity drew us there: Gardiner supplied groceries, gas, and an occasional meal at one of the few restaurants or saloons open during the winter. We never stayed in town long, couldn't wait to get back to the ranch.

But, with our increasing disenchantment with Corvallis and growing enchantment with Yellowstone, we decided to at least consider Gardiner real estate. We went online and found just four houses listed—at prices that made high-priced Corvallis look like a bargain. Forget it, we said. We'll settle into Corvallis again. Won't we?

Mary returned to her music. I put the finishing touches on *In the Temple of Wolves* and published it. Too often we had heart-to-heart talks about how we spent our time and where we wanted to live. While we had a good life, something was missing. We weren't ready to settle for what we had in

Corvallis; we longed for those wild adventures in Yellowstone. Oh, we said, we'll scratch that itch when we return to the ranch for a third winter.

And we did. That third season we went snowshoeing and cross-country skiing with Yellowstone friends. And the quality of wolf watching improved. Though the Lamar Valley wasn't as wolf-filled as the first winter, there were more wolves to see and hear and learn from than during the second. There was also more snow. Much more snow. Too much snow. We spent many grueling days shoveling only to find the paths buried under drifts once again after nights of fierce wind.

By the time that third winter ended, we were certain of two things. First, we would not return for a fourth winter of volunteering. Though we feared losing the connection we had forged with Yellowstone, we had had enough of the duties of a ranch hand. Second, we would return for another winter, but not volunteer. We would simply stay in a Gardiner motel and interact with the town as a community. If that felt good, perhaps we could live in Gardiner during the winters and stay in Corvallis the rest of each year. While that plan excited us, we couldn't help but wonder: If we did not enjoy living in Gardiner *or* Corvallis, what then?

Downplaying our doubts, we returned to Corvallis and picked up where we had left off. Mary played with the band. I spent my days promoting the book and was overjoyed to watch it become an Amazon best seller. As it grew popular, I grew more certain of the debt I owed wolves. If I was going to benefit from writing about them, then I must try to speak for them as well. I got busy learning how to use social media as a platform from which to spread my pro-wolf beliefs and encourage others to speak for these deserving wild creatures.

We arrived in Gardiner for our fourth winter in early December. We made ourselves at home in a small but comfortable, condo-like motel room that overlooked the Yellowstone River. We ventured into the park anytime we wanted. We didn't shovel a single path. We cross-country skied, snowshoed, and watched wolves and other wildlife with local friends. We discovered that Gardiner, though not much to look at, is a friendly community made up of many who shared values similar to ours. We felt welcomed.

About two weeks before we were to return to Corvallis, Mary and I had a long talk. We learned that both of us were enjoying living in Gardiner. We decided to see if we could buy a house for a winter getaway and to rent out the rest of the year.

More places were available in Gardiner this time. With the help of a kind local resident, we found one that we immediately fell in love with. The forty-year-old house with a mountain view sits on a gravel road in a quiet neighborhood. It had recently been remodeled. We so liked the house that we knew we couldn't bear to rent it out to strangers after we stayed there each winter. While we debated incessantly about what to do, we agreed that we had no interest in being landlords. We only wanted to own one house—one we would call home. Locals had warned us that nice houses don't stay on the market long. So, they advised, we had better make a strong offer quickly. By the time we left town, we had closed the deal.

As we drove back to Oregon, we considered all we had to do. We had a larger house to sell and lots of material goods to rid ourselves of. We had family and friends to share our news with and work through their reactions to a decision that might seem sudden but had been years in the making.

Not knowing how the move would turn out led to many distracted days and sleepless nights. We second-, third-, and fourth-guessed our decision. But through that turmoil, one truth stayed constant and clear: we knew that living near Yellowstone was what our hearts craved.

Now that we have lived next to Yellowstone's grandeur for more than a year, we know that making the move to Gardiner was right. But we have also been surprised to learn that Gardiner sits smack in the middle of a number of controversies: the dispute over hunting Yellowstone wolves outside the park; the debate whether wolves help or harm the ecosystem and the local economy; the concern about overuse of and development around the park; the community effort to stop a possible gold mine on the park's border; the outrage over the plan to remove grizzlies from the endangered species list; and the battle to stop the slaughter of park bison.

While living at the Lamar Buffalo Ranch—a wildlife-filled bubble where animals roamed without fear of human intervention—we had stayed blissfully unaware of most of these controversies. But we cannot avoid them in Gardiner, nor do we want to. Instead, we intend to immerse ourselves in the midst of these struggles.

3

The Firing Squad

———

Just two days after Mary and I watched the bison herd fend off the Mollie's in the park, we sit in our car outside the park in a pullout on US 89, that high-speed gauntlet that connects Gardiner and Livingston. We look across the Yellowstone River and the wide, flat, snow-covered Gardiner Basin. Beyond the basin rise low foothills, soft in early morning light. Above them looms the snowy flank and top of rugged Electric Peak.

We take turns scanning with binoculars along the floor of Gardiner Basin to a creek and a thin line of conifers that marks Yellowstone's northern border. Just beyond that border is Beattie Gulch in Gallatin National Forest. There, during the current hunting season, winter-hungry bison that step over the invisible park boundary in search of grass not buried under deep snow are shot by hunters.

Hunter is the wrong word. Those people we watch through binoculars in Beattie Gulch today—there are at least fifty of them, some in camo, some in bright orange vests—are not hunters. They are shooters—a firing squad, really. They stand in the open, within sight of their pickup trucks, their guns ready, waiting for bison to unwittingly enter their field of fire.

Mary and I watch and worry as we count twenty-nine bison, walking in a long line toward the firing squad. The animals seem oblivious to danger. Why shouldn't they be? They spend most of their lives in Yellowstone protected from hunting. As they close in on the firing squad, we hear the first shots, popping sounds at this distance. We are shocked to see a bison fall and amazed that the rest of the herd does not run away. Instead, they circle their fallen member, as if wondering what's wrong. Pop! Pop! Another bison down. Some of the group moves toward the second bison on the ground. Pop! Pop! Pop! Two more bison fall. Still the rest don't flee.

Within minutes, twenty-one bison lay scattered and still in front of the firing squad. We feel some relief as the eight survivors turn from the slaughter and in a much shorter line escape Beattie Gulch and climb up a draw, heading back towards the park. One limps, perhaps wounded.

Mary and I sit silent, sad, and angry. We know that if today's survivors make it back into the park they will be safe for a while. But their days could be numbered. Though these eight escaped the firing squad today, the annual capture of bison by the National Park Service (NPS) at the Stephens Creek Capture Facility within Yellowstone begins soon.

This controversial hunt outside the park and capture within the park are required by the Interagency Bison Management Plan (IBMP). That plan was written in 2000 by a court-ordered coalition of federal and state agencies: the National Park Service, US Forest Service, USDA-Animal & Plant Health Inspection Service, Montana Department of Livestock, and Montana Fish, Wildlife & Parks. Three Native American groups, the InterTribal Buffalo Council, the Confederated Salish & Kootenai Tribes, and the Nez Perce Tribe, joined the coalition a few years later. Goals of the IBMP include confining bison within Yellowstone and reducing the park's population from 5,000 to 3,000 bison.

This winter the plan calls for removing up to 900 bison. At least 300 may be killed outside the park by shooters—like the ones we just saw slaughtered. The bison hunting season lasts about three months. Up to 600 others—which may include those eight survivors—could be captured and interred at the Stephens Creek facility. From that facility, Native American tribal members will haul the imprisoned bison to slaughter houses in Montana. The capture and slaughter begins when the hunt ends and lasts a month or more. All told, the lives of park bison are at risk for at least four months this year.

Managing Yellowstone's bison with confinement and death is done in the name of protecting cattle from brucellosis. The disease can be transmitted from elk or bison to cattle and cause infected livestock to abort calves and ranchers to lose money. But there has never been a documented case of brucellosis transfer from bison to cattle in the wild. Ironically, the transfer originally went in the other direction: cattle transferred brucellosis to bison in the early days of the park when cattle were kept in Yellowstone to provide milk and meat for visitors.

Elk, on the other hand, have transmitted brucellosis to cattle numerous times. But elk are not confined to the park, are not captured and slaughtered like bison. Elk are not viewed as livestock, are not under the control of the Montana Department of Livestock as bison are once they leave the park. Elk are seen as wildlife, as trophies, to be hunted and stuffed. Bison are used as brucellosis scapegoats to be confined and killed.

The IBMP's bison management evokes protests from locals, Montanans, and people all across the United States. This year's protest started a couple of weeks ago in early January, after the hunt began and before the capture started.

Since moving to Gardiner, Mary and I have become drawn physically, emotionally, and intellectually into this life and death struggle. We have joined the Bear Creek Council, a local conservation group where we can work as part of a team of dedicated volunteers to confront the bison controversy. Mary has found news reports and scientific papers detailing the management of bison and elk. I have used that information and our field observations—such as watching the firing squad—to write several articles about the bison slaughter. We have attended meetings where those for or against killing bison speak and sometimes shout opposing views. We have joined about fifty others in a sunset protest march down the main road in Gardiner against the inhumane treatment of bison. The march was organized by Buffalo Field Campaign, a regional activist group that has been fighting for years to end the capture and hunt.

But watching those bison fall this morning is not talking, reading, or writing about senseless killing. This is seeing and hearing it. This is feeling the anger and shock and sadness. This is all too real, and no matter how much we dislike it, the controversial killing will not end anytime soon. Neither will the protest against it.

4

A New Way to Stop

———

The anger and sadness from witnessing bison slaughtered does not quickly fade. Days after that horror show, while I was in the middle of doing something else, I vividly recalled the bison falling to the ground, the rest of the herd encircling their fallen member. The images consumed me. Moments passed until I finally had to physically shake off the memory and force myself back to what I was doing.

When controversy brings pain, Yellowstone's grandeur helps heal. A few days after we were blown away by the brutality of the firing squad, I awaken with visions of cross-country skiing swooshing through my head. Time for some of that grandeur medicine.

After gulping breakfast and packing food, water, and clothes for a full day out, Mary and I drive into Yellowstone, past the Lamar Buffalo Ranch and a pullout filled with early morning wolf watchers. We are almost out of the park before we stop, leave the car, click into skis, sidestep down a bank, and cross a creek on a footbridge.

I should confess that although the availability of skiing was another of the draws for our moving here, Mary and I are by no means experts. After four winters skiing, we still struggle and on occasion fall. We are better at going straight than turning. Better climbers than descenders. Better starters than stoppers. These limitations determine where we ski, since Yellowstone has such a variety of routes from which to choose. We avoid narrow and steep trails that are crowded on either side by trees. We gravitate towards gentler slopes, where we can climb and descend through wide-open territory with few obstacles to crash into.

After the footbridge, we pick up a skier-broken trail and follow it along the flats at the base of a mountain. After a while, we climb through a narrow ravine cut by a stream now frozen and buried under snow. At the top of the ravine, we emerge into a grand valley, bordered on one side by a river and on the other by inviting hills covered with untouched snow. Ah, gentle slopes, wide-open territory, few obstacles. Our kind of skiing.

"Let's go climb those," I say, pointing at the hills with a ski pole.

Mary nods and pushes off. We reach the hills and start up. My breath comes faster, my sweat flows. Wonderful! This is what I've been missing. We remark to each other that we are amazed and pleased at how fast we ascend. When we reach yet another crest, we turn to take in the almost lunar landscape of the snow-covered valley below us. Far below us.

"How did we get this high up?" Mary pants, amazed.

"I don't know," I wheeze. "But to be honest, I'm more concerned about how we're going to get down."

"Well," Mary says, "I'm not going to just point my skis downhill and go for it."

"Hmm," I mutter. "What do I want to do?"

We scan for possible routes; there aren't many. We figure that if we descend by angling across the hills we just climbed, we will decrease the slope and our speed. Satisfied that this is a good plan, we tap poles and get to it.

The plan works until we reach a hill that we can't cross cut because the snow has turned to ice. Our skis will not bite into that ice, and instead of going across, we will just slide down it sideways. Not a good plan. Time to stop and reconnoiter.

"I don't know about you," Mary says, "but I'm going to backtrack until I find a slower and safer way down."

I look at her, then down the hill. Her plan sounds reasonable, but for some reason I still don't understand, I decide to go for the steep and icy descent. Without a word, I yank the tips of my poles from the snow. With the brakes off, gravity pulls me away from Mary and toward that slope of no return.

Behind me, an incredulous Mary shouts, "Are you going down that way?"

My speed increasing, I look back toward her and yell, "I think so..." That's not much of a commitment, but I'm on my way. Time to focus. For a while everything is fine, if a little fast. The snow is soft and quiet and I haven't reached the speed that scares me. Yet.

But just ahead, the sun reflects off the rough surface of snow turned to ice. The glaring patch is maybe one hundred yards wide. At this speed and with my turning skills, I can't avoid the ice. I can stop if I just sit down and let friction do the rest. Or I can keep going. Oh, what the heck, I figure, recalling that old maxim, if you're not falling, you're not learning.

Then the lesson begins. When I reach the ice, the ride gets noisy. My skis rattle instead of swoosh. My legs start to spread when the skis—as predicted—fail to bite into ice. The ride gets faster, and I feel a touch of fear. In response, I tell myself: *Relax. If you just stay upright, you'll go through this quickly.* I settle into the speed and make it across. *That wasn't so bad.* I feel a touch of pride.

But not for long. As my skis go from riding atop ice to sinking into softer snow, they slow. But my body doesn't. Like a tree starting to topple, my nose angles toward the snow. I feel the rush of adrenaline that accompanies full-fledged fear. I flash on a high school physics lesson from many years ago: a body in motion tends to stay in motion unless acted upon by an outside force. Just as I complete the recollection, I smash into the downhill slope. I don't even have time to break the fall with my arms. My head hits first. My sunglasses and prescription glasses go flying. So does my wool hat. My nose cuts a noisy furrow in the snow. I'm reminded again why this is called a face plant. Then I am prone and sliding, my legs and skis twisted like pretzels. My poles, tethered at my wrists, bounce around wildly.

When I finally stop sliding, a body no longer in motion, I pull my face out of the snow, the outside force. Snow covers my eyes; everything's a white glare. I rub the snow away with a bare hand. Bare hand? Where did that glove go? Without glasses, I can't see well, but I am happy to see that I'm conscious.

I lie there and give myself a full body check, what is called a head-to-toe assessment in the wilderness first aid classes we took as part of our training for volunteering at the Lamar Buffalo Ranch. That training would be helpful in situations like this too. Except of course for the essential part of the instruction that I chose to disregard: Avoid situations where you're courting disaster. Working my way from ski boots to hatless head, I determine that nothing's broken or wrenched too far out of shape. I laugh with relief.

Now it's time to get up and find my scattered gear. And get down the rest of this hill. But my legs and skis are so tangled that I can't stand. Finally, I just give up, unclip the skis, and maneuver until I'm kneeling on them. I look around and study the debris field. Is that small bright object over there my prescription glasses? I stand and as soon as I step off the skis, I sink into snow to my knees. Step by cumbersome step I posthole until I reach out and touch the bright object. Yes! Glasses! I'm relieved to find that they're like me: bent but not broken. I gently reverse some of the bend and put them on. Oh, there's that missing glove, and hat, and sunglasses. I collect all three with more strenuous postholing.

I struggle back to the skis and the contortions of getting clipped in. Finally, locked in, fully dressed, and able to see, I'm ready to resume the downhill. The area where I crashed and searched is certainly no longer untouched snow. It looks as if several famished bison have worked it over in search of grass.

I search for the slowest and safest route down—something like the one that I'm sure Mary found would be a smart choice. I pick my way along, stopping often—no more icy slopes for me. When I reach the valley floor, I turn toward the direction from which I expect her to come. I don't have long to wait before I hear the sound of skis approaching. I brush snow off my pants and jacket and stand tall, trying to make myself appear as if nothing went wrong. Mary skis around the corner. The sun and that Yellowstone smile light her face. Until she sees me.

"What the heck happened to you?" she asks, frowning and gliding to a graceful halt.

"Is something wrong?" I ask with the best bewilderment I can fake.

"You've got a bloody scrape on your forehead and your glasses look like they're going to fall off."

Hoping to regain some dignity, I attempt to straighten the glasses. Then I say nonchalantly, "Oh, I just learned a new way to stop."

We burst into laughter that sails across the valley, up those hills, and back again. It feels great to laugh, to revel in the joy of living here, to recharge so I can continue advocating for this wildland and its wildlife.

That grandeur medicine works.

5

The Meanderthals

———

Mary, our hiking partner Leo, and I stand in the morning sun. Our breath mists as it meets below-zero air. We have followed a snow-covered service road to the porch of a locked and shuttered cabin that researchers use in the summer. Beyond the cabin, Yellowstone's Blacktail Deer Plateau fills our vision. We watch in silent admiration as a small group of bison wanders across the plateau and toward a black-snag forest fashioned by one of the many fires that are a natural part of the park's ecology. I'm glad those bison have survived this year's hunt and capture. I hope they stay here all winter, safe from human predators.

Our hiking boots crunch on old, shallow snow as we walk away from the cabin. Little snow has fallen in the few weeks since I learned a new way to stop. Today's plan—if you can call it that—is to hike as far as we want onto the plateau. We hope to see lots of wildlife, maybe even a grizzly bear. This bear management area will be closed in a couple of weeks, by early March, to keep humans and bears separate and safe. If we're going to see a grizzly, today would be ideal. Leo says that one was spotted not far from here a few days ago, after emerging from its den.

Hiking partners like Leo are hard to find. We met him during our first winter at the Lamar Buffalo Ranch, and soon found that his energy and pace match ours. As does his willingness to stop and explore anything, anytime, anywhere. That's what happily turns our hikes into meanders. One day we might hike ten miles. On another day, and in the same amount of time, we might meander four. And learn much more. I call us "meanderthals."

This joy of exploring and learning compelled Leo to leave his well-paid job as a university administrator six years ago. After another marriage that didn't work out, he arrived in Yellowstone determined to stay and build exactly the life he wanted. Like most transplants, he has worked part-time, full-time, seasonal, temporary, and who-knows-how-long-this-will-last jobs. He has lived in all sorts of rentals from a single-wide trailer tucked away in a Yellowstone forest to a cave-like Gardiner hovel with a view of the wall of a metal warehouse. How he makes his money and where he lives is only important to the extent that he does both in or near Yellowstone.

Leo recently realized a long-held dream: he was hired as a Yellowstone guide by one of the best tour companies around. He has all the qualities a guide needs: sharp eyesight, encyclopedic knowledge, a retentive brain, great people skills, incredible passion for the park, and a longing to show others this place he loves.

Within a hundred yards of leaving the cabin, Leo comes across the fresh tracks of a single wolf in the snow. The tracks of the front paws are as big as my hand with fingers outstretched; the rear tracks are a bit smaller. We decide to follow them and see what happens. Such flexibility, after all, is what makes us meanderthals. The wolf's trail disappears into crowded willows, bright in winter red and orange, growing along Blacktail Deer Creek. We plunge into the thicket and spread out. Many of the plants are taller than we are, and we quickly lose sight of one another.

"I've got the tracks of three or four wolves here," Mary calls from my left.

A moment later from my right drifts Leo's reply, "I've got four sets of wolf tracks over here. They're heading toward the ones you found, Mary."

The three of us come together where the tracks join. We smile and high-five at our good fortune. For an hour or more we delight in reading the tale told by the signs of this pack now gone. Sometimes the animals walked together, stepping in each other's footprints. Sometimes, like members of any human family, they went separate ways. One deeper into the willows, another up a sage-dotted hill, some along the bank of the partially frozen creek.

Like the wolves, we split up. I follow a single set of tracks that cross an ice bridge over the creek and climb to a spot where the wolf had bedded in the snow. I sit beside the round depression its body made and admire the view the animal chose. From here the wolf could look across the willow- and conifer-dotted plateau to distant, snowy mountains. It could see anything that moves: a careless grazer, a howling pack mate, a curious hiker.

I arise and follow the tracks back across the creek to where the rested animal had rejoined its pack. I stop, look, and listen for mine.

"I've got a beaver dam here!" Leo calls from somewhere ahead.

Excited about seeing a beaver dam, I weave through the thicket in the direction of his voice. At the same moment that I spot Leo carefully crossing the creek on the dam, I notice in nearby willows the distinctive angled bite marks left by beavers when gnawing off branches for food or building materials. As I cross the dam, I see bite marks and matching angles on the twigs along the structure's top. I stop and spot another dam just upstream. Along these locks created by beavers, the willows grow thick, tall, healthy. Some cradle yet unoccupied songbird nests. Some have soft white buds— spring's coming—growing among stems nipped short by winter-hungry elk or moose.

This combination of beaver dams, healthy willows, and wolf tracks is not coincidental. In fact, there's a controversial theory that describes an important relationship between these three elements. The trophic cascade theory goes like this: In the years between the killing of the last Yellowstone wolf in 1926 and the reintroduction of the first in 1995, the elk population swelled. And with wolves eradicated from the park, proliferating elk could browse wherever they wanted and for as long as they pleased. Willows, as well as cottonwoods and aspen, suffered. With wolves back, the theory speculates, those plants should recover.

This theory has been thoroughly researched and widely promoted by two scientists, Bill Ripple and Bob Beschta. Mary and I know them from Oregon State University in Corvallis, where they teach and Mary worked. In 1997 Ripple learned that aspen trees in Yellowstone had been declining for years. While other researchers had observed the decline, no one could agree on its cause. Fueled by abundant energy and curiosity, Ripple decided to investigate. He analyzed tree growth and found that in Yellowstone's aspen groves seedlings had stopped maturing into young trees about the same time that wolves had been killed off.

Next, he and Beschta studied trees along the Lamar River and found many tall cottonwoods more than seventy years old—trees that would have been young around the time wolves were eliminated. They also found thousands of tiny cottonwood seedlings that had sprouted and grown in the few years since wolves returned. But they found little in between. The scientists concluded that repeated browsing by elk in the seventy years that wolves were absent had prevented seedlings from maturing into full-grown trees.

The trophic cascade theory postulates that the benefits of wolf reintroduction do not stop with healthier stands of willow, cottonwood, and aspen. The benefits cascade deeper into the ecosystem. Where willows are now more abundant, such as where we are meandering along Blacktail Deer Creek, the population of beavers, which love willows, has increased. Where more beavers build more dams, streams grow wider, overflow their banks, and create ponds. The changing waterscape benefits fish, songbirds, insects, and other plants and animals.

Not everyone accepts the trophic cascade theory. I've discussed it with teachers and scientists who work in or pass through Yellowstone. Some roll their eyes at the mention of it, say it's too simple a theory for such a complex ecosystem. Some believe that climate change or fire is a greater determining factor than wolves. But as I look around at this combination of beaver dams, willows, and wolf tracks, the trophic cascade theory makes perfect sense to me.

From my view as a wolf advocate, the theory's relevance is as important socially as it is scientifically. If wolves help ecosystems recover, that's a crucial validation for having reintroduced them. And a strong incentive to encourage the spread and protection of wolves across other ailing landscapes. If, on the other hand, wolves are not essential to ecosystem recovery, then ranchers, with their claims that wolves eat into their profits, and hunters, with their cries that wolves eat their elk, have more ammunition to demand more killing of wolves.

I leave the beaver dam and join Mary and Leo as they follow the pack's trail up a hill. At the top, we dust snow off a couple boulders, preparing to enjoy lunch with a wide-open view. As I kneel and rummage in my pack for food, Leo exclaims, "A moose! Running! Look at that!"

I jump up, stand beside him, and follow his pointing finger that trembles with excitement. In the distance across the creek, a moose has popped out of the willows and is bounding up a slope and away from us. Mary joins us and we watch, astonished at the speed and agility of the animal, sometimes on top of the snow, sometimes postholing belly deep.

"Don't you wish you could move through snow like that?" Mary whispers in awe.

"I wish I could run up a slope like that with or without snow," I confess.

After lunch, we decide to leave the wolf trail and go inspect the tracks the moose left. We bushwhack down a rocky draw, through willows, and across Blacktail Deer Creek before reaching the spot where the moose had sprinted uphill. Leo starts walking in the tracks.

"You need to run like the moose did," I yell.

He laughs and tries to pick up speed only to posthole and slow down. I drop down on hands and knees and scurry on all fours, passing him as he struggles along. "Four legs are definitely better than two." I laugh and kick snow in his direction.

Later, as the sun slides toward the west, we decide to head back. Once in the willows again, we reconnect with the wolf tracks. When we are deeper into the thicket, Mary says, "It smells like a stockyard in here."

A moment later, we find one possible source of the odor: a pile of the partially digested contents of one of the multiple stomachs of a dead bison. This rumen sack is the size of a stuffed backpack. Predators don't eat from these piles, although I've seen ravens and magpies peck at them. We soon find the skull of the bison from which the sack may have come. From the size and shape of the horns, we guess this was a young bull. Our excitement increases when we find in snow near the skull a golden splash of urine containing a small patch of blood, the sign of a female coyote or wolf whose body is preparing for mating. We become downright giddy when we discover just beyond the bison the skull and antlers of a big bull elk, seven points on each side of his rack. In these tall and thick willows, he might not have had much warning of the wolves' approach. He would surely have had a hard time running from them.

As we squat and kneel, inspecting the skulls and inhaling the pungent odor of decay, we grow quiet, less excited. Finally, I whisper to Leo and Mary, "This feels like a graveyard."

They nod their heads in solemn agreement. We arise and replace the skulls where we found them. We head away from the graveyard, out of the willows, and into a small stand of conifers, where the trunks of some trees have been rubbed bare. Dangling from the rough bark bordering the bare spots, clumps and strands of soft bison fur, backlit by low western sun, wiggle in the breeze. Itchy bison have used these trees as scratching posts.

We exit the conifers, cross the creek again, and return to the willows. Mary is ahead of me, Leo behind. Cresting a knoll, I spot the cabin from which we started this meander. Then my attention is drawn to Mary when she snaps her head to the right, stops dead in her tracks, bends forward, and stares. She turns and motions for us to stop. Then she puts a hand to each side of her head and makes a sign for moose antlers: thumbs extended and directed at her head, palms toward us, fingers pointed up and waving. When she turns back to the willows, Leo and I move across the snow toward her, trying to tiptoe so as not to scare the moose away.

When we reach her, Mary points to the willows where we can barely make out the long legs and substantial hindquarter of a large moose. "Jeez," she whispers, "I almost ran into that thing, I was heading right in there."

We have learned that moose are at least as unpredictable as Yellowstone's grizzlies and that we must be careful around them. As we stand there, imagining what might have happened if Mary had been trapped with a spooked moose in those willows, a smaller moose steps from the thicket, glances at us, and begins browsing.

"Wow, how cool is that?" I sigh.

"Oh, that's got to be a calf from last spring," Leo whispers. Though only eight months old, the calf is as big as a small horse.

"The bigger moose must be the mom," I whisper.

If Mary had blundered between that calf and its protective mother, the outcome could have been far worse than just surprising a lone adult moose. We back up a little farther to give mom and calf lots of room—more than the twenty-five yards the Park Service recommends. Since neither animal appears to mind our presence—they haven't changed their behavior—we sit and observe the calf. The youngster looks at us occasionally as it browses. In the silence of wild Yellowstone, we hear the grinding of its teeth and the snapping of willow twigs. Here's another animal whose life has improved with wolves keeping elk from overgrazing willow.

Sitting in the snow in the midst of a recovering ecosystem, the winter-warm sun on my back, a hungry moose in front of me and two inquisitive meanderthals beside me, I grasp how we too have benefitted from the return of wolves.

6

The Last Migration

———

I stand alone in the warm sun alongside Old Yellowstone Trail, the gravel road that connects Gardiner's historic Roosevelt Arch with the park's northern boundary. I only had to drive a few minutes to go from our house to this pullout with its idyllic view. In front of me, the Gardiner Basin nestles between Electric Peak and Sepulcher Mountain on one side and Sheep Mountain on the other. On the basin floor, the road runs down the center, while the Yellowstone River flows along one edge. A mix of many bison and a few pronghorn graze on one side of the road. On the opposite side, a herd of elk grazes.

A week of sunny February days have passed since Leo, Mary, and I meandered with the wolves and moose. Today the temperature is a balmy—and unusual—fifty degrees. Channels full of snowmelt reflect the sun as they flow and froth and head for the river.

As I have done on many days over the last few weeks, I'm going to spend the next hour or so driving the five miles of Old Yellowstone Trail that cuts through what I have come to call the kill zone. The road leads straight to the heart of the controversial management of bison by capture and killing. I will drive slowly and stop often. I want to observe the bison and their migration. As best as I can, I seek to understand this controversy from their point of view.

I start by taking a few steps away from the car and dropping onto all fours. The ground is cool and moist. I study the close-cropped vegetation. Emerging through the dead debris of last year's growth are scattered blades of new grass, no more than an inch tall. Those tiny green shoots and the lack of snow are what drives Yellowstone's bison to walk the forty or so miles from the Lamar Valley to here. They leave their home range because deep snow or an ice layer makes reaching the dried grass there impossible. This grass means survival.

If allowed, the bison would continue their migration out of the park and into Paradise Valley to the north. Though heavier on grass and lighter on snow, Paradise Valley is not paradise for bison; it's parceled into ranches and ranchettes, some owned by residents who—for fear of brucellosis or property damage—don't want to share their pastures or backyards with bison.

While bison migrate here to survive, death awaits. They may be shot just outside the park like the twenty-one that Mary and I watched fall to the firing squad. Or they may be captured by the Park Service and sent to slaughter.

I stand, brush dirt from my hands and knees, and look out at the distant NPS Stephens Creek Capture Facility that mars the edge of this pastoral scene. Mary and I were driven into that facility in a big yellow NPS bus a couple of weeks ago. Once out of the bus, we toured the facility with a dozen members of the media and conservation organizations. Mary and I had volunteered to represent Bear Creek Council on the tour. Our group was accompanied by armed park rangers because of the Park Service's fear of possible civil disobedience at the facility. The tour was led by a Park Service spokesperson and a couple of bison biologists. They aimed to explain the ins and outs of the capture process.

Over the course of the morning, we learned what capture entails. When the bison graze near the facility, Park Service employees on foot or horseback approach the animals and direct them toward an open gate and into a large pen. Once entrapped the animals are hazed to a processing area. There, a machine holds each frightened bison in place while an NPS biologist jabs the wide-eyed animal with a needle and draws blood that will be tested for brucellosis. A Montana Department of Livestock sticker with a number and bar code is slapped on the animal's side, like a product being readied for display. Park Service employees force the bison into various holding pens, where some will battle against other trapped animals and cause injury.

A day or two after capture the bison will be hazed out of the pens and into the trailers of several Native American tribes. They are then hauled to a slaughter house. The locked and loaded trailers are accompanied by a Montana Department of Livestock vehicle with an armed officer behind the wheel. If an accident occurs during transit and bison somehow escape the trailers, the officer has orders to shoot them dead. This is quite a statement about how rabidly the Department of Livestock opposes bison roaming outside of Yellowstone. Once processed at a slaughter house, the meat and hides will be shared among tribal members.

I turn from the view of the capture facility and walk back to my car. I pull onto the Old Yellowstone Trail and drive in the direction of the facility. Less than a quarter-mile later, I stop to watch twenty bison—calves and their mothers, a couple of yearling males—graze alongside the road. The low winter sun creates a halo above the light brown fur along the back of a nearby calf.

These bison were led here by matriarchs who learned this migration route from matriarchs that came before. Along the way, bison often walk in the plowed road. This conserves energy and gives them a better chance to win this yearly struggle between starvation and spring. If they have any thought of the danger that awaits them near the park boundary, their desire for less snow and more food overwhelms it. Plus, they have only been captured in Gardiner Basin since 1996. Perhaps not enough time has elapsed for the awareness of danger to have been passed down from one wise matriarch to the next.

Migration comes naturally to bison. In fact, migration is how we came to have bison here at all. Two to three million years ago, a much smaller animal in southern Asia began moving north and evolving, according to Harold Picton in *Buffalo Natural History and Conservation*. They migrated to what would become Siberia and crossed the Bering Land Bridge to Alaska. They turned and followed their noses south through the Yukon to the Great Plains. There they grazed with mammoths, mastodons, and camels, according to Michael Punke, in *The Last Stand,* his book about the saving of bison. Big saber-toothed tigers and dire wolves hunted those bigger grazers. And eventually so did our early ancestors. Many of those huge mammals became extinct, perhaps because of human hunting, perhaps because of climate change. Yet the ancestors of Yellowstone's bison survived. Their migration of millions of years and thousands of miles ended here in Yellowstone.

But by 1901, poachers had taken all but twenty-three of the park bison. Now, after one of the first and most successful wildlife restorations in the world, Yellowstone has healthy herds in the Lamar and Hayden Valleys. And when deep snow locks away their food, these bison do what they've always done: migrate. Group by group they head for Gardiner Basin and the kill zone.

I park in a muddy pullout that offers a closer view of the Stephens Creek Capture Facility: a long brown barn, scattered smaller outbuildings, some trailers for hauling animals, a hodgepodge of NPS vehicles, and lots of tall bison-proof fencing. On other days, I have observed from here that most bison graze within a mile of either side of the facility entrance road. Once I counted eighty in a long line that pointed right at the capture facility. With a ridge rising to their left, it would be easy, I imagined, for NPS employees to haze the bison toward the gate in the nearby capture pen.

Today, near the entrance road, thirty-five bison graze and rest, letting their incredibly efficient digestive systems squeeze all the nutrition possible out of a winter diet of dried grass that has, according to one biologist, the nutritional content of an empty cereal box. This is yet another adaptation—like migration—that has made bison such survivors. If cattle were left to fend for themselves in Yellowstone's winter conditions, they would perish.

Leaving the pullout, I motor along until I come to a big female bison standing like a crossing guard in the middle of the road. I stop, roll down the window, and smile at the singing of distant coyotes and the croaking of a raven in flight just overhead. The bison looks back at her calf and grunts. The calf, horns short, energy high, responds to the mother's message and bounds across the road, head swiveling from me to its mother.

The bison's ability to reproduce is another of the species' strengths. Females may conceive their first calf when they are two to three years old. They will then produce, according to P.J. White, Rick Wallen, and David Hallac in their book, *Yellowstone Bison,* a single calf every one or two years for the rest of their lives. That means each female could add up to ten offspring to the Yellowstone herd. An NPS spokesperson on the tour told us that one reason for each winter's bison kill is to offset the birth of calves from the previous spring.

The crossing-guard mother and her energetic calf join a group grazing in and around a field of boulders, some as small as bowling balls, others as large as compact cars. Millennia ago, these glacial erratics hitchhiked atop and inside glaciers that crept into and covered this basin, following the course of the Yellowstone River. When the melting glaciers deposited their erratics here and ended the last ice age, an unknown number of ancestors of these grazing bison roamed this continent.

Thousands of years later when Euro-Americans arrived, at least thirty million bison—a conservative estimate— roamed North America. Bison could be found, says Punke, as far east as what would become Washington, D.C. Based on what I've heard and seen over the last month, Yellowstone's bison could use a representative or two in D.C. about now.

I drive away from these members of an ancient species among ancient boulders and arrive at the entrance road to the capture facility. Looking down the long entrance road, I count twenty bison marching along it, as if to turn themselves in. Today they are safe: the capture hasn't started yet, and they can't go in.

Neither can I; the road is marked with a sign that reads "Authorized Personnel Only." When Mary and I were bussed down that road for the tour, the spokesperson and biologists told us that the Park Service does not want to capture and kill park bison. But they must comply with the IBMP plan that requires this lethal management approach. NPS officials say they are searching for a life-saving alternative, but ranchers and Montana's Department of Livestock are powerful opponents to a more humane and sensible treatment of these remarkable survivors.

Putting the capture facility behind me, I continue on toward the park's northern boundary. I steer through a dogleg and then stop in the road near an interpretive sign surrounded by bison. The colorful sign explains that Native

Americans arrived here about 11,000 years ago. I assume they sought then what these bison seek today: shelter from winter and food to keep them alive until the warmth and bounty of spring return.

I navigate another dogleg past some grazing pronghorn and reach a stretch of road where I recently counted thirty-five bison. They had migrated past the closed capture facility and were moving toward the park boundary where shooters could be lurking less than a mile ahead. Fearing for the bison's safety, I rolled down my window and yelled "Go back!" But they kept walking, drawn, I imagine, by the desire to graze on the tiny blades of new grass growing between the road and the Yellowstone River.

I continue on to a little pullout on the left, the last within the park. Just beyond this pullout is the parking lot for the trailhead at Beattie Gulch. The lot is used by hikers in summer and bison shooters—like the ones Mary and I saw—in winter.

A few nights ago, Leo and I attended a solemn ceremony in that parking lot with thirty-one others, including several Native Americans. The ceremony was led by Buffalo Field Campaign staff. We stood in a large circle under a half moon that shone through thin clouds and lit the snow on the surrounding mountains. A chilly wind blew from the direction of the park, the same direction from which bison come and unknowingly enter the kill zone. The wind carried the smoke and scent of the glowing ceremonial bundle of sage we passed around the circle. Each holder of the sage could speak his or her mind or heart or simply pass. Most spoke; everyone listened. Some in the circle called the bison their brother or sister. With smoke and hope, words and emotion, we sanctified this place where bison are slaughtered.

Today, in the middle of that same parking lot, a man skins a bison that hangs by its rear legs from a hoist mounted in the bed of a worn pickup truck. The truck sits less than fifty feet outside the park. Some of the bison's orange fat is still attached to the carcass. I am shocked by the sight of what I know is just another of the hundreds of bison that will be taken this winter. I don't want to watch this butchering, but this gruesome finale is part of the controversy I'm trying to understand. I bring out binoculars and watch the man work; he appears confident and skilled. Two other men watch, occasionally pointing at the bison and making comments I can't hear.

When I can stand no more, I leave the pullout and the park and drive toward the deadly center of the kill zone. About a quarter-mile beyond the hanging bison, three pickup trucks sit on the side of the road near a gate. That unassuming gate controls access to a well-graded road used by members of the firing squad to drive their trucks closer to bison they have killed and need to load. To access this road, the shooters must obtain a permit from tribal game wardens or state game wardens. Beyond the gate, ravens fly and land and fly again, carrying away scraps of butchered bison.

———

Based on figures available as of this writing, shooters killed 356 bison just outside the north entrance to Yellowstone that winter. They killed another twenty-four just outside the park's west entrance. An additional fifty or so were wounded but able to retreat to the park—like the one that Mary and I watched. However, their wounds were so serious that the fifty had to be killed by park employees. Another ninety-seven bison were captured at Stephens Creek and shipped to slaughter. Finally, fifty-seven calves and yearlings were captured and contained, not sent to slaughter. Four of the calves died while in captivity. The rest were held in hope that a proposal will be approved and they can be shipped to the Fort Peck reservation where they will live out their lives as members of a captive herd.

7

Observation Point

When we lived and volunteered at the Lamar Buffalo Ranch and needed a mid-season respite from work and visitors, we would take a snow coach to the Old Faithful area and stay a couple of days. Since our move to Gardiner, we plan to continue that tradition of a mid-winter trip.

Now, as February draws to a close, we want to escape from the heartbreaking reminders of the ever-present bison controversy. We need a break from meetings where critics and supporters debate the value of these majestic animals. We are weary of seeing bloody leg bones of bison killed by shooters along the forest service road near our house. We want to quit fearing what the final bison body count will be this winter. And we would surely like to reduce the frustration that comes from feeling powerless to stop the inhumane slaughter but compelled to try.

Early in the morning, we gather our backpacks, snowshoes, and skis and drive the six miles to Mammoth Hot Springs. At the hotel, we check in for our reserved seats on a snow coach, a twelve-passenger van that travels on tracks instead of tires. In winter, the road from Mammoth to Old Faithful is closed to cars but open to these coaches.

We climb aboard the fully booked coach, squeeze into our seats, and settle in for the ride. Snow is everywhere along the fifty-one-mile route—sparkling in valleys, draped on mountains, pillowed atop riverside rocks, and decorating the backs of stoic bison standing in steaming thermal areas. I marvel at the hardiness of these animals and silently command them to stay where they are, far from the kill zone.

When we arrive at Old Faithful, overstimulated and exhausted from the three-hour trip through wonderland, we register and settle into our cabin. After dinner we set our alarm for 5 a.m. and crawl into bed.

The next morning, refreshed and excited, we leave the warmth of the cabin and step off the porch onto packed powder. The temperature hovers a few degrees above zero. In the glow of our headlamps, diamonds glisten on the snow's surface. We round the corner and walk hand in hand past other cabins, windows dark, occupants sleeping—as most reasonable vacationers are before first light.

"Wow, it looks like my breath is actually freezing when it hits the air!" Mary exclaims in a whisper. She tilts her head skyward, forms an "O" with her mouth, and puffs three times. A trinity of white circles drifts, expands, and vanishes into the black, star-speckled sky.

We continue beyond the Snow Lodge along a path bordered by knee-high snow. We pass the general store and gas station, both shuttered for winter. We cross a snowy road, rough with tracks from yesterday's snow coaches and snowmobiles ferrying excited visitors, most of them day-trippers. Once beyond the visitor center, our insulated boots crunch on snow-free gravel, a testament to the subterranean heat that produces the dependable eruptions of Old Faithful, murmuring just ahead.

When we reach the walkway that borders the geyser, we stop and scan. The cones of our headlamps, moving left and right like searchlights, illuminate not another soul. The Upper Geyser Basin is all ours—exactly why we set the alarm. I aim my beam at a nearby bench and tug at Mary's sleeve. Her light melds with mine and reveals the perfect impression of a visitor's rump in the six-inch deep snow atop the bench. We chuckle; another day of snow tracking begins.

Mary's light swings skyward into the mist rising from the thermal features. "It's really steamy here in the basin," she says. "I can't see the stars anymore."

I point in the direction of a low shadow rising into darker sky. "How about we head up to Observation Point?"

"Let's do it!" she says, forging ahead.

I catch her and we follow the tunnel of our headlamps along the wide, empty boardwalk, its snowy cover tracked here and there by winter's sparse visitors. What a contrast to summer. Then, when an eruption nears, this would be standing room only, abuzz with excited comments in many languages. Last year a record-breaking four million visitors crowded into Yellowstone; most made sure to visit Old Faithful.

Leaving the walkway, we turn onto the narrow half-mile trail that climbs through lodgepole pine to Observation

Point, a small viewing area tucked into the forest above the geyser basin.

"Well, at least I'm not postholing," Mary says. "Looks like we won't regret forgetting the snowshoes back at the cabin."

We laugh at our forgetfulness and pass through glittering clouds of elated breath. Mary leads the way as we settle into a pleasing procession, the silence broken only by the rhythmic crunching of our boots. When I turn off my headlamp, Mary's down-clad figure is silhouetted against the glow of her lamp. I look left and right, admiring how snow-flocked pine branches reflect the light. Then I walk right into Mary, now stopped in the middle of the trail.

"Sorry," I mutter and back away. Silent, she seems not to notice. I shrug and return to my tree gazing.

A moment later she points her finger downward and whispers, "Look at this."

I move beside her; we bend forward. I click on my headlamp, and our beams converge on a track.

"That's a dog type of print," Mary says.

She places her gloved hand, fingers spread, beside the smaller track. Then, with her index finger, she touches the triangular indentation in the snow at the rear of the track. The triangle's point reaches the center of the track. The four elongated, oval indentations above the triangle are each as big as the tip of her finger. At the front end of each of the four is a dot where a claw pierced the snow.

"Coyote, I'll bet," she says.

My beam bounces as my head nods. "Yeah, remember how we ran into one last summer when we took this hike before dawn?"

Continuing to climb, we spot fresh coyote scat. "Looks like he's heading up this trail, too," Mary observes.

We kneel, inspect the scat, and find fur and bone fragments within. We stand, brush snow from our knees, and move on. A few paces farther ahead the tracks of a hare cross the trail.

"Wow, he's in a hurry," I say. "There's about five feet of untouched snow from one track to the next."

"And the coyote tracks don't follow them," Mary adds. "Looks like that guy may have sensed Mr. Coyote and beat feet."

Eager to create more stories—a favorite pastime of ours in winter when tracks are obvious and plentiful—we study the snow. Pointing, I follow small tracks that start at the base of a lodgepole pine, cross eight feet of snow, and materialize along the top of a downed tree. "Squirrel, I bet."

Mary spots a trail of even smaller tracks that disappears into a miniature snow cave under the root ball of the downed tree. She drops onto all fours and maneuvers her head into the cave. "Maybe a mouse," she says, her voice muffled. "It's insulated by snow and even has grass to nestle into." She stands and claps snow off her gloves. "Nice digs."

Leaving the track tales, we continue upward and reach Observation Point. We lean against a wooden fence that runs along the edge of the overlook; our hips touch comfortably. The sky is just beginning to lighten. We turn off the headlamps and allow our eyes to adjust. In the distance below, the Upper Geyser Basin steams, surrounded by the Firehole River on one side and a clutter of Park Service buildings on the other.

"There's the Big Dipper," Mary says, pointing straight up.

"And a flashing planet off to the west just above the horizon," I offer.

As I try to recall the name of the planet, Mary leans in close and whispers, "Listen…you can hear an eruption in the basin."

I pull my hood down and push the wool cap from my ears. I catch the rumble and splash of one of the many geysers that make Yellowstone a natural marvel and led to its becoming the world's first national park. I point to a gray column undulating against darker sky. "Look at Old Faithful getting ready."

Our gloved hands find each other. I squeeze hers gently. She squeezes back. No words. Our silent communion is speech enough.

A moment later we hear a sound like someone cannonballing into a pool. We have seen Old Faithful produce that sound when a short, pre-eruption column of water gushes out and then smacks down around the cone. A soft hissing follows as the runoff slides toward the river. Finally, a quieter splash signals when the steaming drops join the Firehole.

By the time those drops flow thousands of miles to the Gulf of Mexico, we will be back in Gardiner, immersed again in controversy, this winter retreat over, this moment but a memory. For now, we're here, warm with the joy of being just where we want to be, together and alone in the grandeur of Observation Point in winter. Our own reinvigorating tradition.

8

Saving Yellowstone's Bison

———

Since 1985 more than 7,000 Yellowstone bison have been killed. Almost all were either captured at the Stephens Creek Facility and sent to slaughter or killed by shooters just outside the park, according to White, Wallen, and Hallac.

I find this killing of Yellowstone's bison appalling for three reasons. First, park bison are genetically pure—they have no cattle in their DNA. They have not been bred to be sluggish or docile. Slaughtering that precious genetic resource makes no sense.

Second, the reservoir of this ancient animal is too shallow to drain. Of the thirty million bison that once roamed the West, only 5,000 or so now survive in Yellowstone. Instead of shooting or slaughtering bison as a means of controlling the park's population, we could ship some elsewhere to build other herds and increase our national mammal's population and range.

Third, killing threatens to undo the hard work of George Bird Grinnell and the many other determined people who saved these bison from eradication more than 120 years ago.

The story of saving Yellowstone's bison began on a fall night in 1893 when Ed Howell and his partner left Cooke City, Montana, and snuck a ten-foot-long sled bulging with supplies past a government patrol cabin in the northeast corner of Yellowstone. Pulling the sled, the two tough poachers skied south to where some of the last remaining wild bison in the Lower 48 were hiding. Howell and his partner made camp in remote Pelican Valley beside Astringent Creek.

Their plan, according to historian Aubrey Haines in *The Yellowstone Story*, was simple: kill all the bison they could find, remove their heads, and hang them in trees to protect them from scavengers. The two men would then wait for spring when they could bring in packhorses, haul their bounty out, and sell the heads for up to $300 each. (That was a lot of money; the average wage at this time was about $10 per week.) But after an argument, Howell sent his partner packing. Alone, he settled into his tipi to await the morning and what he hoped would be the start of a profitable winter.

It's hard to imagine this scene happening today, but in the early years of the world's first national park, there were few staff and even less money to protect wildlife. The nuts and bolts of a wildlife protection policy—the who, what, when, where, and why of protection—was a work-in-progress. Meanwhile, an increasing number of news reports and photographs of park wildlife encouraged some dubious characters to grab their rifles, get to the park, and gun down some animals. Why not? There were no laws to prosecute them, and poaching was profitable.

Ed Howell was just one more in a long line of poachers profiting from bison. In 1875, three years after Yellowstone became a park, scoundrels slaughtered scores if not hundreds of park bison and moose. Most of that slaughter was not for food, says Haines; usually just tongue and hide were taken. Park officials recommended prohibiting hunting, but nothing came of it.

To make matters worse, the hunters laced the carcasses they left behind with strychnine to kill wolves and wolverines that dared dine on the remains. Other scavengers died as well. This common practice—approved by Philetus Norris, the park superintendent—may have led to the extermination of Yellowstone's wolves by 1880, "rather than by 1930, as is commonly believed," argues historian Paul Schullery in *Searching for Yellowstone.*

By February of 1894, Howell had killed "at least six and possibly fourteen or more buffalo," according to Michael Punke. But he was running low on supplies and returned to Cooke City to stock up. His passage left tracks found by a scouting party of soldiers. (The army was in charge of the park from 1886 to 1918.) The tracks headed toward Cooke City, which concerned the soldiers. The mining town just outside the park's northeast entrance was known as a haven for poachers—and winter was poaching season.

When the soldiers reported the tracks to park superintendent Captain George Anderson, he had reason to share their concern. Three years earlier Anderson had learned that a local taxidermist had mounted the heads of several Yellowstone bison. Anderson investigated and captured the Cooke City poacher, E.E. Van Dyck, who had supplied the heads. Anderson had his man, but all the captain could do was stretch his legal power and make an example of Van Dyck. He legally confiscated the gear Van Dyck had used while poaching and illegally held him for a month in the Fort Yellowstone guardhouse in Mammoth Hot Springs. A year later, Anderson captured another Cooke City bison poacher, held him in jail for a short while, and confiscated his property. With poachers fearing little punishment, Yellowstone's bison suffered: in just one year the herd shrunk from 500 animals to about 250.

When Captain Anderson learned of the sled trail leading toward Cooke City, he sent soldiers to investigate. On the morning of March 12, 1894, a soldier named Troike and a civilian scout, Felix Burgess, left the Lake Hotel where they had spent the night. They skied into a terrific snowstorm.

Early the next morning, the two found six bloody bison heads hanging like obscene ornaments from a tree in Pelican Valley. They continued investigating, according to Anderson's report, and came upon an encampment, the snow marred by human tracks. While searching the camp, they heard six shots. They skied up a nearby hill and from that vantage point saw a poacher about 400 yards away with five dead bison around him. They watched as the man, with his dog standing nearby, began removing the head of one of the bison.

Troike and Burgess wanted to capture this poacher, but had to weigh the dangers involved. The first consideration was their firepower—or lack of it. The two had only one weapon, an army-issue revolver. The distance between them and the poacher rendered the revolver useless. The poacher, on the other hand, had a dog that could warn of their approach and a rifle powerful enough to kill bison and accurate enough to kill two distant and careless men.

Their other challenge was the snow. Though the scout and the soldier were experienced skiers, they could hit a patch of crusty snow and break through with a crunch that would resound in the silence of the valley. The noise could alert the sharp-eyed poacher, who might then spot the intruders floundering in deep snow and shoot them. If ever accused of the crime, he could claim that he acted in self-defense, since there would be no witnesses to contradict him.

Regardless of the risk, scout Burgess took the revolver and started skiing quickly across the wide-open valley floor. As he closed the distance, the wind grew loud, the snow stayed quiet, the dog remained oblivious, and the poacher continued decapitating. With just fifteen feet to go, Burgess pointed the revolver—a lethal weapon at that distance—and shouted for the poacher to put up his hands and surrender.

Ed Howell was caught bloody-handed on March 13, 1894, the nation's first capture of a poacher in the act. The scout, the soldier, and the poacher began the long ski—at least forty miles over wild winter terrain—to the guardhouse in Mammoth Hot Springs. Howell's punishment began immediately; his captors made him break trail—a brutal job in deep snow.

When Captain Anderson learned of the capture, he was overjoyed with this public relations coup, according to author Jeff Henry. Coincidentally, Anderson was hosting a dinner with journalist Emerson Hough, who, along with photographer F. Jay Haynes, was part of a group exploring Yellowstone for the influential New York weekly magazine *Forest and Stream.*

Captain Anderson arranged for Hough and Haynes to meet the poacher at a patrol cabin, near present-day Norris Hot Springs. There, Howell bragged to the journalist that his punishment for killing those bison would be nothing more than expulsion from the park and forfeiture of gear worth less than $30. Hough sensed a story and wrote the tale of the thrilling capture of unrepentant Ed Howell. Haynes set up his camera; the captors and poacher posed. The story was telegraphed to *Forest and Stream.*

Hough's account of a crime without punishment reached the magazine's editor, George Bird Grinnell, a renowned and experienced conservationist who had already fought for almost twenty years to protect wildlife, especially bison. He was familiar with Yellowstone, having visited the park as an impressionable twenty-six-year-old in 1875, in the company of an army survey party.

Grinnell vowed to do more than just publish one story. Instead, he peppered *Forest and Stream* with Hough's updates on Howell's case. He included Haynes' photographs; for the first time Americans saw images of bison killed by poachers. But Grinnell didn't stop there. He wrote editorials demanding Congressional action. He encouraged readers to write to their representatives and complain that no laws existed for punishing Howell and other Yellowstone poachers. Once the national press picked up the story, enraged citizens inundated Congress with letters and petitions.

But Grinnell still wasn't satisfied. Well-connected, he gathered influential friends and headed to Washington, D.C. There they told the tragic tale of the slaughter of wildlife by poachers with no fear of retribution. Their powerful presentation and the public outcry did the trick: on March 26—just thirteen days after Howell's arrest—Representative John Lacey of Iowa introduced a comprehensive bill in the House of Representatives. The Lacey Act prohibited hunting, killing, wounding, or capturing any bird or wild animal in Yellowstone. It called for appointing marshals to make arrests and a commissioner to decide punishment. It authorized funds to build a jail.

While Grinnell publicized the capture and Lacey introduced his bill, Captain Anderson had to deal with Ed Howell. Anderson again resorted to the only tools he had: illegally holding Howell in jail for a month and then legally kicking him out of the park with orders to never return without permission.

On May 7, 1894, a few weeks after Howell was released from jail and left the park, the Lacey Act—which had sailed through the House and Senate—was signed into law. Poachers like Howell could now be arrested, prosecuted, and legally jailed—not just expelled.

For a while, Howell honored his expulsion. But the lure of Yellowstone was too great, and in late July—just two months after passage of the Lacey Act—Howell returned. The park superintendent, writes Haines, found Howell in

Mammoth Hot Springs "coolly sitting in the barber's chair in the hotel." He arrested him on the spot—for returning without permission—and hauled him off to jail, once again.

This time Howell received more than a slap on his wrist. On August 8, Ed Howell made history for the second time when he became the first person to be convicted under the Lacey Act, the law his poaching had helped pass. He was sentenced to a month in jail and fined $50—about $1,250 in today's currency.

This battle to save Yellowstone's bison, orchestrated by George Bird Grinnell and fought by many others, was the first national showdown over the environment. This was, says Michael Punke, the first time our nation made "the conscious decision to protect wildlife and wild places when it cost something..." The Lacey Act saved the lives of Yellowstone's few remaining bison and went on to become the foundation for law enforcement in all our national parks.

I can't help but wonder what George Bird Grinnell would say about the capture and slaughter of Yellowstone's bison at the Stephens Creek Facility. What would he say about the hazing, the blood draw, the bar codes, the holding pens, the injuries, and the slaughter of the descendants of bison he worked so hard to save? What would he say about killing bison that step just beyond the park boundary? What would he say about our moonlight attempts to sanctify the area where bison die?

Perhaps he would say something similar to what he wrote in 1883 in an opinion piece in *Forest and Stream*. "Every citizen shares with all the others the ownership in the wonders of our National pleasure ground, and when its natural features are defaced, its forests destroyed, and its game butchered, each [citizen] is injured by being robbed of so much that belongs to him."

Those words ring as true today.

Spring

9

Bison Babies

———

It's late April, and Mary and I are in the park in search of bison calves. We have heard that newborns have been sighted, and we want to see them. We have driven forty miles, to and through the Lamar Valley, and while we have found some lone bulls, females with calves have been surprisingly absent. At the confluence of the Lamar River and Soda Butte Creek, we turn around and, hoping for better luck, start the return trip to Gardiner.

After we cross over the Yellowstone River on our way to Tower Junction, I catch a glimpse of what might be a group of bison in the distance. Desperate for a sighting, I pull over to the side of the road and park near where I hope they might eventually cross.

While waiting, Mary and I contemplate the landscape, a study in Yellowstone's exquisite arrival of spring. New, bright green grass crowds the side of the road. Yellow wildflowers and white, black, and red rocks accent the fields. A bit farther from the road stand olive-green and winter-weary sagebrush. Then comes dark green conifers, bold against the clouds building up and hinting at more of the rain that fuels this celebration.

I catch movement from the corner of my eye. An adult female bison climbing the roadside bank comes into sight. Another follows. My excitement mounts. "Do you think it could be…?" I let the question dangle. Another adult arrives. "Oh, this just looks like more adults. I don't see any…"

"Babies!" Mary exclaims, pointing and cutting short my lament.

Like magic they appear. First, one beside its mother, its back barely as high as its parent's belly. Then, more moms, more babies. One mother stops and drinks deeply from a tiny stream fed by recent rain and melting snow. The calf stands and watches but doesn't drink. As more bison gather in the road, I count fourteen adults and seven calves. I open the window and listen to the light clicking of their hooves on blacktop, a sound that doesn't match the animals' massive size.

Mary and I point and laugh. For us, these babies signal spring's arrival and something more. These beauties with their curly red-orange hair, their long legs, and their big black eyes that see the world anew are living proof that Yellowstone's bison population will recover from another winter of the brutal capture and hunt.

As the babies stand in the road, each calf only inches from its mother, it's easy to see how they differ. The calves don't yet have the prominent shoulder hump adults exhibit. That crane of muscle and bone will come later and enable them to swing their big adult heads and plow up to eighteen inches of snow from life-sustaining dried grasses. The calves don't yet have the bouffant hairdo some adults sport. The calves are not the same color; they won't begin turning brown until July.

"Hey, wait a minute," Mary says, again pointing. "Is that a shriveled umbilical cord dangling from that calf's belly?"

I look at the calf. "Huh, it is. And there's another with a cord, too. These calves weren't born very long ago."

When born, each weighs between thirty-three and sixty-six pounds. Once a calf slides out of mom and onto Yellowstone's soil, things begin to happen quickly. Within thirty minutes, the calf can stand and nurse. Within one week, it can eat grass, drink water, and start learning which other plants to eat by watching its mother. Within seven to twelve months, it will be weaned and have developed the large digestive tract with multiple stomachs that make bison superior to cattle, deer, or elk at wresting sustenance from winter's dried grasses.

I smile at the sight of one calf nestling its black nose into its mother's pantaloons, the long fur of her legs. It's hard to imagine this tiny and helpless animal growing to 2,000 pounds if a male and 1,100 pounds if a female. It's also hard to imagine, as we watch these calves wobble along, that one day they will be able to sprint at thirty-five miles an hour, turn on a dime, and hurdle a five-foot-high fence.

Once mature, these calves will produce another generation. While almost all the females will become mothers, the males will not be as successful at becoming fathers. When five to six years old, the uninitiated males must win the right to breed. The contests occur from mid-July to mid-August, during the rut, a time when thousands of bison cover the Lamar Valley floor. Older—and wiser—males grunt, bellow, and roar challenges to claim females and deter other suitors. If attitude, posture, and uproar don't deter a competitor, it's time to rumble. Two contestants will dodge and feint and then butt heads and shove each other with their powerful legs. An experienced battler may slam a contender in the side with his big head and sharp horns.

At some point, one of the fighters will call it quits. Both loser and winner can sustain injuries. One study found that 50 percent of bulls inspected showed fractured ribs that likely occurred during rut battles.

On the road beside us, a calf, its new body still perfect, kicks up its rear legs and bounces down the road ahead of its mother. The mom grunts. The calf stops, stares at her, and returns. The mother and calf then cross the road in front of us with the other bison. We notice that a couple of the adults are starting to shed their winter coat. It's time for them to start rubbing.

One March morning at the Lamar Buffalo Ranch, Mary and I were awoken by the trembling of our log cabin. Curious, I slipped out of bed, threw on a pair of pants and a jacket, opened the door, and stepped onto the small porch. As I looked around, the rattling of the structure continued, and I heard a grunt from one side of the cabin. I took a couple of cautious steps and eased my head around the corner.

Shocked, I found myself face-to-face with a big bull bison that was using the side of our cabin as a rubbing post. His massive head was about four feet away and he looked at me as if to say, *Hey, can't a guy rub in peace?*

I slipped back around the corner and opened the door, to find Mary sitting up in bed. I pointed toward the wall where I had encountered the bison. I gave her the signal for bison: thumbs touching each side of my head and index fingers pointing straight up. As I rubbed against the door jam, the big bull generated another tremor. When Mary returned the sign of bison and nodded her head vigorously, we burst into laughter.

While a log cabin will do as a rubbing post, rough-barked trees are favored. The other day in Hayden Valley, home to another bison herd, I counted thirty trees in one stretch with large, bare bison rubs.

While some of the mothers crossing the road are starting to shed, others have ribs showing under their fur. They have spent all winter nourishing a growing fetus while subjected to below-zero temperatures in wind, snow, and sleet. Fortitude isn't free: the mothers have barely won that race between starvation and spring. Now, as Yellowstone greens, they must eat and rebuild their fat and strength. While adult bison have the need and stamina to graze ten hours a day, calves need time to rest. Recently, on our way back from Old Faithful, we had to maneuver our car around a prone calf sleeping on the warm blacktop, surrounded by a small group of adults. Formidable protection for a youngster's nap.

In a few more weeks, Mary and I will return to watch these calves play, running and jumping and kicking up their small hooves. That play develops their physical strength and teaches them the rules of the herd. One rule they should learn quickly is to not stray far from the group. Hungry grizzly bears and wolves may pick off stragglers. Though a mother will fight to defend her calf, she has limits. Under the commonsense rules of nature, it's better for the herd if the mother withdraws, loses the calf, and saves her own life, so she can produce offspring later.

As the calves mature over the next few years, some will die from the trauma of a hard winter, from falling through thin ice of a lake, colliding with a vehicle, or giving birth. But adult bison, with their large size, sharp horns, incredible speed and agility, and willingness to defend one another, lose few members to predators, as we saw a few months ago when a group repelled that invasion by the Mollie's pack. As the regulated capture and slaughter prove, man is the only predator that bison need to fear.

The adults and calves are heading away from the road, silhouetted against a sky that is now clear and blue. In a moment, they will drop out of sight behind a sage-covered hill. A busy time awaits them. By early summer, this group of twenty-one, an average size for this time of year, will join other bison and form a group of about 200. By the beginning of the rut, that group will merge with others and form a herd of 1,000 or more in the Lamar Valley.

Once the breeding ritual is complete, the bulls will go off to spend winter alone or with a few other bulls. The females will merge back into smaller groups, each led by a matriarch. The pregnant females will carry their calves through the ravages of winter. Then after nine to nine-and-a-half months, the babies will come, once again heralding spring and proving that life indeed goes on.

10

A Grizzly Courting

One morning near the end of May, Mary, Leo, Karen, and I leave Yellowstone's Fawn Pass trail and bushwhack upslope toward the 8,002-foot peak of Terrace Mountain. Halfway through a stand of conifers, I spot long, vertical scratches on a tree trunk. Could those be the claw marks of a grizzly bear? Excited, I wave over my hiking partners. We scrutinize and debate and finally agree that the marks—so high on the trunk—are from a big grizzly. We look at each other and smile; wouldn't it be great to see a grizzly today? Mary and I are especially hopeful, having spent most of our time in Yellowstone during winter when bears are tucked away in dens.

After one last look at the claw marks, we continue bushwhacking upslope. Entering a clearing, we stop, turn, and gaze out across Gardner's Hole. In the middle of the basin sits Swan Lake. Farther still is a wall of snow-covered peaks, part of the Gallatin Range. Some of them, Bannock Peak, Antler Peak, Mount Holmes, and Trilobite Point, reach over 10,000-feet high. Though the view captivates, clouds have formed, cooling the morning. Time to move on and warm up.

We follow a narrow animal trail: the hoof prints of bison, elk, and big horn sheep mix in soil free of snow and soft from spring rain. To the chatter of a squirrel's alarm call, we high-step through a crisscross of downed timber and then slalom between short young pines.

We reach a small meadow covered with dried grass flattened by the now-vanished snow of last winter. Through the pale golden remnants sprout this year's green, only inches high, but likely what drew the grazers up the trail. Yellow, purple, and white ground-hugging wildflowers decorate the meadow. While Leo and I wander the clearing in search of more bear sign, Mary and Karen drop to their knees to admire and identify wildflowers.

Mary and I bonded with Karen in our winters of working with her at the Lamar Buffalo Ranch. When the two of us arrived at the ranch for our first winter, green as could be and anxious about how we would handle our rookie season, Karen was also there for her first winter. But she was a confident and skilled veteran of seven busy summers. At the end of each school year, science teacher Karen would climb into her car, drive from her Central Oregon home to Yellowstone, and become volunteer Karen. Once retired from teaching, she decided to volunteer in winter as well.

Whether we were cleaning cabins, shoveling snow, driving buses, or cross-country skiing, Karen took the time to teach us much about the ranch, Lamar Valley, and Yellowstone. But what really impressed us was not just her knowledge, but her contagious love for the park. That love called her back to all those busy summers and quieter winters. She has returned again to the ranch as this summer's interim manager. But before becoming consumed by that job, she wanted to join us on today's hike.

Leaving the meadow, the four of us climb until we reach a large, flat area. From here we can see Bunsen Peak, the colorful remains of an ancient volcano. We are staring at the same view that Mary and I enjoy from our dining room window, but it's much closer, close enough, it seems, to touch. We stand silently for a moment, in awe of this peak, just one of many—at least seventy other named peaks over 8,000 feet decorate Yellowstone. Then we turn and survey the distant floor of Gardner's Hole, a quilt of light and dark green, enhanced by Yellowstone's ever-changing interplay of clouds and sunlight.

Beside me, Mary asks, "What's moving out there? Is that a bear?"

I swivel my head in her direction and find her squinting in concentration. She raises and focuses her binoculars. I wait for those sharp eyes to find the target.

"Yes. Yes, it is!" she says and jabs a celebratory fist into the air.

"Where?" Leo implores. "*Where?*"

Mary directs Leo and he zooms in his binoculars. "I got it!" he yells. "That's a big grizzly. It's running. Look at those muscles rippling! And there's a smaller one to the right."

"One's light and one's dark," Mary notes.

Their play-by-play captivates Karen and me as they describe how one bear stands, the other bear sits, then both grizzlies run or join in what look like playful movements.

"Think they're looking for elk calves?" Mary wonders aloud.

"I think it's a male and a female," Leo says. He watches for a moment and then adds, with excitement in his voice, "Oh, yeah. That's courting behavior."

The mating season for grizzlies begins in mid-May and can last until mid-July. Since June is just around the corner, the dance has begun, and we are watching the first of the four steps in grizzly mating that Jim Halfpenny describes in *Yellowstone Bears in the Wild*.

Courtship, the step we are viewing, started recently when this male smelled the female coming into heat. Having sniffed that she may soon be ready to mate, he has followed her closely day and night. They may stay together for more than a week, and he will drive away other suitors. Right now, though, we see no challengers.

During the next step, rejection, this smaller female may discourage the hopeful, larger male, by sitting, growling, swatting, biting, or slipping away. She may encourage other males.

If he overcomes her rejection, he will slide into the acceptance step and try his best to mount the female. But she may not cooperate. He may fall off and swat her, and she may swat him back. This step may look as much like fighting as flirting. If he loses interest, she may nuzzle him to rekindle the fire and keep the dance going.

During the final step, copulation, this male may fertilize an egg in this female, but the egg will not implant right away. It will go dormant and float in her womb, where it waits to implant.

If all goes well, by as early as late September, this female will be pregnant—from this male or possibly several other suitors—and enter her den. If she is healthy and well fed, the fertilized eggs will finally implant, and one to four cubs will begin developing. By late January to early February, while the snow flies, wind howls, and temperatures fall outside, she will give birth inside the den to hairless and sightless bundles of joy, each weighing about as much as a can of soda. While she sleeps, the cubs will nurse and grow. From when she entered the den till the moment she and her now five- to ten-pound offspring emerge, almost six months will have passed.

If she and her cubs stay within the confines of Yellowstone National Park, they may live a long life. But I fear for their safety once they venture beyond the park's invisible borders, if the US Fish & Wildlife Service (USFWS) delists all grizzlies in the Greater Yellowstone Ecosystem from the Endangered Species Act (ESA).

Their plan to delist has been controversial from the day it was announced. If delisting occurs, it will be challenged in court by scientists and conservation organizations. I will root for a successful court decision. I don't want to see bears—like these two and any cubs they may produce—at the mercy of Montana, Wyoming, and Idaho, the three states that surround Yellowstone. The governors, legislators, and fish and game departments of these states have enacted wildlife management policies that have wasted another Yellowstone icon, wolves.

Hunters, ranchers, and state and federal employees have killed thousands of wolves in Montana and Idaho since their 2011 delisting. In Wyoming once wolves were delisted, so many were shot that the federal government realized Wyoming's Wolf Management Plan was not a plan to conserve wolves; it was a plan to kill them. They could be killed almost anytime, anywhere, and for any—or no—reason. Some of the wolves shot—such as 06—had unknowingly stepped from protected Yellowstone into Wyoming's free-fire zone. In 2014 wolves were returned to Endangered Species Act protection in Wyoming.

But wolves are once again targets in Wyoming, since a U.S. Appeals court ruled that the state's wolf management plan is acceptable. And if a few politicians have their way, wolves will again be targets in Minnesota, Michigan, and Wisconsin, other states with large wolf populations. One proposed bill would delist wolves in those states from ESA protection and block concerned citizens from challenging the delisting in court. Conniving politicians aim to cut all judicial review, checks and balances be damned!

Given the immediate and ugly slaughter once wolves lost ESA protection, I have no doubt that unprotected grizzlies will die too, as cash-strapped fish and game departments rush to bring in fees from trophy hunts.

Mary and I attended a meeting where Montana Fish, Wildlife & Parks (MFWP) staff presented their grizzly hunting plan for public comment. This meeting occurred *before* grizzlies were delisted. MFWP staff revealed that the USFWS required the creation of such a hunting plan and that their Idaho and Wyoming counterparts were concocting plans, too. The three states have already divided up the bounty with each promised a certain percentage of the bear population.

The USFWS will sit back and watch the slaughter happen. You only have to look to Idaho's brazen killing of wolves to understand that all the USFWS demands for a no-longer-protected species is an annual report and a minimum number of breeding pairs. Other than that, Idaho can do as it pleases. That has included spending $2 million of Idaho taxpayer money over a span of five years to eradicate wolves. And hiring federal gunners to shoot wolves from helicopters. All this killing comes after the USFWS spent millions of federal tax dollars to increase the wolf population.

Given this recent history, the USFWS must know that delisting is a death sentence for hundreds of the very grizzlies they have worked so hard to recover. And they certainly know that for every scientific argument to justify delisting, concerned scientists have a valid counter-argument.

Here's one example: the USFWS claims that the decline in cutthroat trout and whitebark pine nuts, two of the grizzly's primary foods, does not threaten the animal. But concerned scientists warn that grizzlies, who are omnivores, will simply resort to eating more meat. Scientists predict that the grizzly's increased need to find meat will lead it to attack livestock—especially on public lands. And that will lead straight to conflict with humans. If hungry bears are no longer federally protected, hungry bears will die.

As I attended meetings and read reports where the delisting was presented and challenged, I found so many examples of this point-counterpoint that I wondered: if every reason for delisting the grizzly is so readily challenged, why delist now? Why not wait until the rationale is clearer and more widely accepted by a majority of scientists?

I didn't have to look far for an answer: Perhaps Dan Ashe, USFWS director, wants his legacy to be that the agency he ran excelled in saving endangered species. When the agency announced their intention to delist the grizzly bear, their press release concluded: "The Obama Administration has delisted more species due to recovery than any prior administration…"

The only way Director Ashe can take credit for saving endangered species is to remove animals from the list. This time it's the grizzly bear; but other species will soon find themselves without protection.

Ashe's ambition may be only part of the problem. He may also have lost control of an agency that should be basing such life-and-death decisions on science but isn't. Before Ashe announced his plan to delist the grizzly, the well-respected Union of Concerned Scientists surveyed scientists in the USFWS and three other federal agencies. Almost three-quarters of those surveyed at USFWS believed that political interests receive too much consideration at their agency. Almost half of USFWS scientists expressed concerns about industry interference in agency decision-making; that's the highest percentage of the four agencies surveyed.

The Union of Concerned Scientists went so far as to recommend that the USFWS take steps to increase scientific integrity and decrease political interference in the agency's scientific decision-making. Given the controversy in the debate over Ashe's decision to delist the grizzly, that recommendation seems to have been ignored.

I hope that the conservation organizations that band together and hire lawyers will succeed in challenging the delisting. I have learned through advocating for wolves that much conservation happens in courts. Court battles aren't cheap, and Mary and I will contribute what we can to help fund the battle. We know many other concerned citizens will do the same. A study by the Humane Society of the United States and Wyoming Wildlife Advocates found that more than two-thirds of Americans oppose opening up a trophy-hunting season on grizzlies in Idaho, Montana, and Wyoming. Only 20 percent support trophy hunting.

With the future so uncertain, I fear for the safety of these two grizzlies in the early stages of courting, and I fear for the future of offspring they may produce. I want grizzlies to increase their range and numbers. For that they need Endangered Species Act protection. Without that protection, I hope that these bears, all of Yellowstone's grizzlies, stay within the park's boundaries. Those invisible lines are the only real protection they have.

11

Life Changes for a Wolf Pack

———

Mary, Leo, and I start at the same trailhead from which we had bushwhacked north to the top of Terrace Mountain just a week ago. But today we intend to go south, farther into Gardner's Hole, the valley where the grizzlies were courting.

We are just minutes from the trailhead when we hear wolves howling, distinct high and low notes creating a captivating chord. We stop and listen. With no discussion, we head away from the trail and toward the howling. No destination is more important than listening to wolves and maybe even seeing them. As we bushwhack in their direction, the only sounds are our excited breathing and our pants legs rubbing against knee-high sage. Then comes the rough call of a sandhill crane from the same direction as the howls.

I crest a rise, look down at the ground, and find a large, fresh, pile of bear scat. We are standing in the area where the two grizzlies courted. The landscape is wide open, so I'm not worried about surprising a bear. But still, I take a longer and closer look around. You can't be too cautious.

To my left, I hear Leo direct Mary, "Look on the ridge, on the skyline near those three snags. There's a black wolf."

Following his directions, I squint and try to pull in the ridge—it's about a mile away. The black specks that I distinguish there could be a wolf or a rock impersonating a wolf. I pull out my camera and zoom in. It's a wolf, sitting with ears perked and its attention focused to its right. I spot another wolf standing and staring at a nearby sandhill crane—probably the one that gave the call. I'm amazed by the large size of these cranes. Standing on its long legs, this bird's eyes are at the same height as those of a wolf.

The wolves howl again. From the south comes a coyote alarm call, a series of loud barks, warning packmates that danger lurks nearby. These primal and ancient sounds draw the three of us together. We stand, shoulders almost touching, reveling in the music of the wild.

The wolves are on a ridge that protrudes into this valley. Just below the ridgeline, and running much of the length of the ridge, is a narrow snowfield—still hanging on at the end of May. The wolves are heading toward the snow, and the three of us cheer them on in whispers. As we know from observing wolves in winter, they'll be much easier to see against that white backdrop.

When the wolves reach the snowfield, we count them. A gray and four blacks saunter along in a line, noses to the snow. The gray and one of the blacks wear collars. As I study them, I see that the gray is smaller than the blacks and has a rat tail, one devoid of fur. Three of the blacks also have rat tails; only one black does not. I wonder aloud if the wolves have mange. Leo thinks they don't, but we all agree they have lost some fur.

"That's the 8-Mile pack," he says. "Or at least some of it. I've heard there are nine wolves in the pack this year."

The 8-Mile pack did not originate within Yellowstone, although they are descendants of the wolves that were reintroduced into the park. Their name comes from a creek in Paradise Valley, where the pack originated. But the pack often travelled between Paradise Valley and the park. This pack's history, as taken from Yellowstone Wolf Project annual reports, reveals much about how life can change for a wolf pack.

In 2011, the pack denned here in Gardner's Hole and produced ten pups. By late summer many of the pups had mange; only one survived the year. Complications from mange may have taken the rest. Still, by the end of that year, the pack had ousted the shrinking Quadrant Mountain pack from this territory.

Perhaps the 8-Mile wolves decided to stay in Yellowstone to avoid the pressure of being hunted. When traveling between the park and Paradise Valley, they must pass through territory in which they could easily end up as trophies, since wolves are hunted in Montana.

On the ridge, one of the rat-tail blacks takes off, loping out of the snowfield, through the sage, and up onto the ridgetop. Another follows. We watch the two bound along the ridge, disappear down the other side, and then reappear on top. We don't know if this run is for prey or play, so we start bushwhacking in the direction they are heading, hoping we might be lucky enough to see them bring down an elk. When we reach the base of the ridge, all the wolves have gone down the other side and beyond our view. If we want to see what they're up to, we'll have to climb.

Mary stares at the steep muddy slope in front of us and asks, "We're going to climb that?" Then she laughs, looks at Leo and me, and says, "Let's go!"

Though the ridge doesn't require our dropping to all fours, there are times when I come close to doing so. At the top, we stop to catch our breath. I turn a slow 360, taking in landmarks I recognize from other hikes. In the direction we came from, Swan Lake mirrors a gray sky. A few other unnamed ponds dot the valley floor between us and Bunsen Peak, its top shrouded in clouds. Continuing my turn, I look along the flat top of Terrace Mountain, from which we watched the grizzlies courting. Next comes the gentle green slope of the back side of Sepulcher Mountain. Then massive Electric Peak, rough and pointed, and slashed with snow. Finally, there's Quadrant Mountain, a long sloping peak that forms one majestic border of the Gardner River basin. What a backyard we have! I'm happy that Gardner's Hole—only ten miles from our house—is beginning to feel as comfortable as the Lamar Valley did when we lived there.

During 2012, our first year at the ranch, while we spent hours watching the thirteen wolves of the Lamar Canyon pack, the 8-Mile pack—with seven adults—strengthened their claim to Gardner's Hole, forty miles away. The pack was led by a large black male (871M—any wolf that wears a radio collar is given a number to assist biologists in identification and data gathering) and the same gray female (909F) that we see with the pack today. The pack had as many as six pups during that summer but ended the year with only three. Two other pack members were killed by hunters just outside the park in Unit 313. Despite those setbacks, by the end of the year the 8-Mile pack dominated Yellowstone's Northern Range—the wildlife-filled grazing land that makes up about 10 percent of the park. They had expanded their turf onto Mount Everts and parts of the Blacktail Deer Plateau, where they outnumbered their neighbors.

While staring into binoculars, Leo asks, "I wonder where those wolves got to?"

"They could be anywhere by now," says Mary, scanning left and right.

I study the basin floor for movement. The Gardner River forms a series of oxbows bordered by red, yellow, and orange willows. Farther from the river, sage abounds. Between the sagebrush, short spring grass creates a varied—and vivid—green. I see nothing moving.

Then, a howl. As one, we pivot in the direction of the sound.

"I got him," Mary whispers. "Across the river, just below that large snow bank, in that light yellow grass. A black. He's lying down and howling."

"Maybe he's calling the others," Leo says.

"It's as if he's calling us," Mary says with a giggle. "We're over here you three," she sings in a barely audible wolf-like howl.

Near that black, I catch a glimpse of the gray alpha female. The wolves are again about a mile away and at that distance she blends into the sage. But when she steps in front of red willows, she becomes obvious. Soon we have spotted all five wolves. Most are stretched out in the grass, bedded down after a busy night. If there are nine wolves in the pack now, where are the rest? Perhaps they are back at the den with this season's pups.

We decide to sneak to another hill that is lower but closer. To get there, we keep a stand of conifers between us and the pack and climb the other slope. As we near the top, the three of us crouch low to reduce our profiles. At the top, we squat instead of stand. When we look toward the wolves, the gray is looking right back at us, as if to ask, *What took you so long?* So much for sneaking up on animals that make their living sneaking up on animals.

In 2013, when Mary and I spent our second winter at the ranch, the Lamar Canyon pack had splintered after the death of the alpha female. Meanwhile, the 8-Mile pack, with nine adults and nine pups, had grown to be the largest in Yellowstone. In the world of wolves, the size of your pack matters. The mighty 8-Mile pack continued to expand its territory, taking turf from smaller neighboring packs. But the wolves were rarely observed. Unlike wolves in the wide-open Lamar Valley, the 8-Mile wolves spent much of their time in parts of Gardner's Hole that were far from park roads—and roadside wolf watchers. That's still the case, and one reason our experience today feels so special.

The wolves seem untroubled by our presence; they make no effort to move away. We decide to mosey on toward the river and sneak a bit closer. We enter a conifer forest, the dark lightened by bird song. We crunch through snow that covers the ground in patches. Moments later we emerge from the forest onto a small hill overlooking three ponds. The view of the ponds, Gardner River, and Gallatin Mountains, all accompanied by the loud serenade of chorus frogs stops us.

Mary breaks the silence. "There's elk out there grazing."

Leo turns his binoculars in the direction she points. A moment later he whispers with force, "There's a black wolf near them! On the ridge to their right."

Fascinated, we watch the elk register the presence of the 8-Mile wolf. Three of the five bulls, their antlers thick and brown in velvet, raise their heads and track the wolf's progress. The wolf shows no interest in this potential meal. Perhaps the pack has returned from a successful hunt. The wolf passes the elk and moves in our direction; we are downwind and it cannot catch our scent. When it disappears from sight behind a hill, the elk resume grazing.

We resume observing and locate the rest of the pack. There's the gray alpha again watching us watching her. Sun glints off her eyes, her gaze intense even at this distance. A moment later she dismisses us, averts her stare, and ambles behind a large boulder, disappearing from sight.

"There's that black again," Mary says. "It's following the gray's scent."

The rest of the pack is sitting and laying about. We decide to stroll toward the river.

In early 2014 when Mary and I returned for our final volunteer winter, and the shattered Lamar Canyon pack had only two wolves remaining, the 8-Mile pack was still the largest in northern Yellowstone. Three of the 8-Mile females produced sixteen pups. But this would be the high point of the pack's ascendancy. In October, the alpha male was killed by a neighboring pack. And, as had happened with the Lamar Canyon wolves, the 8-Mile pack splintered. At least seven wolves left and formed the neighboring Prospect Peak pack. By the end of that year, the 8-Mile pack, still led by the gray female that just dismissed us, had shrunk to seven adults and two pups.

As we hike toward the river, Leo says, "Look at this. It's the skull of a bighorn sheep."

We kneel down to inspect the find. The skull is white and weathered. The curved bones that create the big horns are speckled with brown. The sheaths that once covered the horns are missing. The big empty eye sockets gape. There is a large hole that once housed the nose. Though the lower jaw is missing, the upper teeth show little sign of wear. This was probably a young animal.

"What in the heck was a bighorn sheep doing out here?" Mary asks, gesturing with a sweep of her arm to indicate the floor of the wide-open river valley that surrounds us.

Leo points across the river to a rocky cliff on the side of Quadrant Mountain and says, "I wouldn't be surprised to see bighorns there." He pauses, looks like he's imagining scenarios. "Maybe the wolves found the bighorn when it came to the river to drink. Perhaps they chased it farther into this valley and away from the cliffs."

We won't answer the questions our adventures today have asked, and that's just fine. The many mysteries—solved and unsolved—that we encounter on our meanders add to the fun. We continue on.

A few moments later, Leo exclaims from behind us, "Holy smokes, a bear skull."

Mary and I race back to where he stands, treasure in hand. "I've never seen one of these in the wild," he whispers in awe. Neither have we, and we share his wonder. After we each caress the smooth, large, white skull, Leo gently replaces it where he found it, and we move on toward the river. We pass a mule deer skull with antlers attached.

We climb another hill. This gives a grand view of the Gardner River winding through the basin. In the grass at our feet, we discover a sheath from a bighorn sheep. This sheath would probably fit over the bones in that skull we studied a few moments ago. Bones and antler fragments lay scattered everywhere, but these are not pieces from a single carcass. These are of many ages, and all are less than a foot long. Just the right size, I figure, for young wolves to carry here and gnaw on while the pack rests on this high ground and scans the territory for the next meal or trespassing wolves.

By early 2015, the paths of the Lamar Canyon and 8-Mile wolves finally crossed. The alpha male of the small and struggling Lamar Canyon pack had been killed by other wolves. The Lamar Canyon alpha female had begun associating with a couple males from the Prospect Peak pack, the one formed by wolves that had split from the 8-Mile pack a year earlier. The 8-Mile pack still had nine wolves, but it had not grown from the previous year and was no longer the largest in the park.

We descend to the river and make this is our lunch spot. I can't believe that four hours have passed since we heard the first howl. In all that time, we spent just a few moments on the trail; the rest of this trip has been a wild bushwhack. We have been living in the present, aware only of what was around us, unaware of the pasing of time or miles. A perfect meander.

As we sit and eat, the 8-Mile pack rests in the grass about a mile away. They seem to tolerate our presence as long as they maintain that buffer of space. After lunch, I lay back onto the grass. As I stare through now-heavy eyelids into blue sky, I can't help but laugh. We and the wolves are acting the same: relaxing on a fine spring afternoon in Yellowstone.

12

Saving Four Wolves

———

On a lovely June evening a few days after we meandered with the 8-Mile pack, Mary, Leo, and I walk through the double doors of the Gardiner K-12 School. We are here to attend a meeting on the proposal to increase the quota in Montana Wolf Management Unit 313 from two wolves to six.

Unit 313, bordering Yellowstone and Gardiner, is the unit the 8-Mile wolves pass through when traveling between Yellowstone and Paradise Valley. Other wolves enter the unit when they follow prey out of the park. A wolf does not know the location of the boundary line of Unit 313. But hunters know exactly where the line is, and when wolves have crossed it. I wish members of the 8-Mile pack could attend this meeting; this political process will affect their lives and the lives of other Yellowstone wolves. We hope that many pro-wolf people will come and speak for them.

Since we are a few minutes early, the three of us sit in the hall near the principal's office and wait. As others arrive, we hug or shake hands, happy to see friends and allies. I'm reminded of the Mollie's wolves greeting each other as they prepared to sort and sift the bison herd.

When the start time nears, we walk down the hall and into the school's multipurpose room, abuzz with conversation. At the front of the room behind long folding tables sit six staff from Montana Fish, Wildlife & Parks (MFWP). Sam Sheppard, a regional supervisor, anchors one end. To his left is a note taker with a laptop and four MFWP biologists.

These biologists recommend the number of wolves that hunters can kill in Unit 313. Montanans and out-of-staters then comment on that recommendation. Ultimately, the Montana Fish & Wildlife commissioners vote to decide a quota—the one recommended or some variation. If the process of setting the quota sounds straightforward, it isn't. But the end result is: wolves are killed.

Killing a single wolf that happens to be an alpha can splinter an entire pack, as it did with the Lamar Canyon and 8-Mile wolves. Keeping the quota in Unit 313 at two wolves instead of six will not only save the lives of four wolves, it could actually save four wolf packs. That's worth fighting for.

In the multipurpose room, three long rows of cafeteria tables are set up for the public, with about thirty people already seated at them. Leo, Mary, and I choose a place in the middle of the front row. Also in the front row, but much closer to the door sits one of our elected local officials. I heard him propose at a previous public meeting an increase of the quota to six.

I then scan the faces in the front and middle rows of tables. I see people I know; most don't want the quota raised. Many are Gardiner residents with economic as well as personal reasons for protecting wolves. Some are Yellowstone guides with clients that want to view wolves in the wild. Some own businesses that depend on ecotourism. As Doug, a local who sells spotting scopes to wolf watchers, tells it, no one buys a scope to watch dead wolves.

A number of wolf watchers sit at the middle table. Some make the pilgrimage every year, even a couple times a year. Some come from far away. I admire their dedication; they have taken time away from a precious park visit to attend this meeting tonight and support the wolves they so dearly love.

I look at the third row of tables. I don't recognize many of the people sitting there. Some wear camouflage vests, pants, or hats. I assume that most of the back row wants the quota increased. I make eye contact with a few and nod. One looks away. A couple nod back.

The chance to look anti-wolf folks in the eyes is one big difference between my advocacy in Gardiner and my advocacy in Oregon, where I wrote online posts, sent emails and letters, and signed petitions. Another difference is that here in Yellowstone, I can also look wolves in the eyes, as I did with that intense alpha female of the 8-Mile pack.

I glance behind and to the left of the back row. On the edge of the raised stage with closed curtains sits Dan Vermillion, his feet dangling. He is the chair of the Fish and Wildlife Commission and has made it clear that he will vote to increase the quota from two to six. Politically savvy wolf advocates figure he is maneuvering behind the scenes to rally other commissioners to vote with him.

To the right of Vermillion, an armed county sheriff, arms crossed, leans against the edge of the stage. Another armed officer stands beside him; I can't tell where he's from. Do they have a personal interest in the wolves, or are they here to head off trouble?

At a previous public meeting held in May to discuss raising the quota, no law enforcement attended. Mary and I—and a number of other Gardiner residents I see in this multipurpose room tonight—made the three-hour round-trip to the MFWP office in Bozeman. At the front of that office, in a large meeting room, a TV showed split-screen images of other MFWP meeting rooms across Montana. A small camera near the TV focused on a podium where people could comment and be seen and heard by Vermillion and the other Fish and Wildlife commissioners sitting in Helena. I had silently commended MFWP for their use of technology, allowing Montanans to meet virtually. Otherwise, our drive from Gardiner to Helena would have required a six-hour round-trip.

Before that May meeting, I had spoken with Marc Cooke, president of Wolves of the Rockies. His organization and others have worked tirelessly and successfully to reduce the quota in Unit 313. Cooke told me that one Fish and Wildlife commissioner had convinced two other commissioners to reject the proposal to kill six wolves. Those three commissioners needed wolf advocates to attend the May meeting, speak out, and show that the public supports their contentious decision.

Responding to rallying emails from the Bear Creek Council, Wolves of the Rockies, and a number of other conservation organizations, many supporters attended. The commissioners rejected the proposal to kill six wolves. Walking out of the Bozeman meeting room in May, I felt we had won a victory, believed we had saved four wolves, maybe four packs. But I'm new to Montana and didn't understand how this would all play out.

In reality, that May meeting did not end anything. Instead, it started a mandatory period of public comment on how many wolves—if any—should be killed. Once that comment period ends in about two weeks, MFWP biologists will read all submitted comments and then decide whether to submit another quota proposal to the commissioners. Finally, in July, the commissioners will vote again. *That vote* will be final.

As we sit tonight at cafeteria tables in the multipurpose room of Gardiner School, we're a long way from saving four wolves.

At the front of the room, Sam Sheppard rises from his seat to start the meeting. He walks to the front of the staffer table and leans against it. The room quiets. Smiling, Sheppard greets us and asks that we be respectful of each others' opinions. He explains that his staff is here to listen to our comments, not to have back-and-forth discussions with us.

A man in the back row raises his hand and says with a hint of frustration, "So does that mean we can't ask questions?"

Sheppard, maintaining his even tone, tells him questions are permissible but the meeting will not be a back-and-forth between staffers and attendees. Then he opens the meeting for public comment.

After a few people speak, Bonnie, a representative of the Sierra Club, stands and says, "People come from all over the world for a once-in-a-lifetime chance to see a wolf in the wild, and that chance is undeniably reduced with hunting on the park borders, as we saw in a recent study." She adds that last year hunters and trappers killed more than 200 wolves in Montana.

A man in the back row stands and says he was born and raised in Gardiner. For his entire life, his family has worked as outfitters—helping clients hunt wildlife. He believes that tourism in Gardiner to see wolves in Yellowstone "should not dictate what we do with Montana wolves in the 313 area." He seems to frame this controversy as the federal government bullying the state of Montana—a position western conservatives take on many political issues.

"This is Montana," says Sheppard, breaking his own rule on the back and forth. "This is not Yellowstone National Park North." He explains that the park operates on a preservation model—wolves aren't hunted in Yellowstone. But Montana uses a conservation model—wolves are hunted.

Sheppard adds that there is room within Montana's model for considering what he calls "social values." I feel encouraged to hear an MFWP supervisor say this. Sheppard's biologists have already stated that the wolf population in Unit 313 could biologically recover from the loss of six wolves. But can the residents and economy of Gardiner withstand that loss? That's the social value.

Another man from the back row says, "If wolves stay in the park, we won't affect them at all."

"The fact of the matter," replies Sheppard, "is that animals don't recognize political boundaries. This species [wolves] is linked to the elk. That is their primary grocery and they're going to follow the groceries."

Shauna, a Yellowstone guide sitting in the front row, explains how the killing of 06 affected her income: she lost more than $2,000 in tips after that one wolf was shot. Her comment creates a buzz in the back row and generates a few minutes of back and forth between pro- and anti-wolf attendees, until Sheppard puts both hands into the air and quiets the room. "This," he repeats, "is not going to be a back and forth."

From the back row, another man asks angrily, "So we can't ask questions?"

Sheppard brings both arms across his chest and states firmly, "There is not going to be dialogue going back and forth among the audience."

The room falls silent except for the rustle of three men in the back row whom I assume are members of the anti-wolf congregation. They stand up, tug at their baseball caps, and march out. Watching them go, I figure they did not come to have a productive conversation; they came here to fight. They will never agree with protecting wolves. They want wolves gone. And when wolf hunting season arrives, they will make their opinion known with bullets. An attitude like that makes a small quota all the more essential.

After the three leave, a man who spoke before from the back row breaks the silence with a diatribe against the

Sierra Club's political influence. He sounds as if he sees this controversy as the Sierra Club overpowering Montana's Fish and Wildlife Commission.

When he finishes, Ilona, a wolf advocate and chairperson of Bear Creek Council's wolf committee, asks Sheppard, "Can we allow everyone in this room to make their first comment before we go to second comments?"

"That's fair enough," says Sheppard with a nod.

Doug, who sells spotting scopes, asks Sheppard if we can have a simple show of hands of how many people support the two-wolf quota as opposed to six.

Sheppard shakes his head and says, "I value everyone's comments, but what I've found in the past is that if there is an overwhelming majority, that may silence some people." He pauses and then adds that the staff wants "to hear what people think and have to say."

From the back row someone yells, "Shoot the wolves!" While this prompts laughter in the back row, it draws concern from the middle and front rows. Is there any way, I wonder, to bridge such a chasm?

Linda, co-owner of a local ecotourism business, stands and says that she too suffered financially after 06 was shot. When the Lamar Canyon pack scattered, there were fewer wolf sightings, and that led to fewer wolf watchers. Her business income was off for two years.

Then Mary stands and turns so she can look Commissioner Vermillion in the eyes. She smiles and, referring to the May meeting in Bozeman, states, "I'd like to thank the commissioners for making the decision to retain the two-wolf quota for 313, though my preference would be to reduce the quota to zero." She addresses the rest of her comment to Sheppard.

After she finishes, I want to applaud her statement of conscience. The reality under Montana law is that there cannot be a buffer zone, a permanent zone around Yellowstone where zero wolves are taken. There can only be a quota that is subject to change. Only three small units in the state have quotas. Unit 313 and one other border Yellowstone. The third unit borders Glacier National Park. Anywhere else in Montana allows the combined maximum hunting and trapping bag limit of five wolves per person during the current season.

After a couple more people speak, I stand to comment. Inspired by Mary's statement, I start with, "I would like to see the quota in 313 at zero wolves, not two." Bowing to reality, I add, "But if you have to go with a number, then I would go with two." I encourage the MFWP biologists to establish a management goal that recognizes tourism and research as a priority for setting wolf quotas near Yellowstone and Glacier. This is an idea Ilona shared with me in one of our many conversations concerning wolf management.

After I sit down, Doug remarks that watching wildlife instead of killing it can be compared to catch-and-release fishing. In catch-and-release, "Fishermen get the sport. They catch the fish but they let it go." In wildlife watching, photographers and watchers get to see and enjoy the animals, while the animals survive to provide similar experiences to other wildlife watchers.

Nathan, chairperson of the Bear Creek Council and co-owner with Linda of an ecotourism business, stands and says that he too was raised in Gardiner. He graduated from the Gardiner School. Having any wolves killed in 313 "is like Russian roulette. You don't know if the wolf that is killed is one that is going to be known to wolf watchers and tourists." He recalls the boycott of some Gardiner businesses after 06 was killed.

Nathan's comments draw opposition from a man in the back row. "There's probably a lot of folks who weren't here or who don't remember that once upon a time Gardiner was a much more thriving town that was busy all summer, all fall, and a good portion of the winter." He looks around the room and adds, "There are a lot of us who have lost economic stability due to the lack of management [of wolves]..." He refers to a time when elk hunters with guns boosted Gardiner's economy. Now the money comes primarily from ecotourists armed with spotting scopes and looking to catch and release wolves.

Judging by the comments tonight, when it comes to the economic impact of wolves, the pro-wolf and anti-wolf sides share little common ground. One side says that their incomes fall when wolves *are* killed. The other side says that their incomes fall when wolves *are not* killed.

Sheppard comes close to the front row of attendees, stops and scans the faces before him. He appears to be composing himself. Then he nods as if giving himself permission to speak. "Across the state of Montana, wolves are an accepted part of the landscape, much more so than here. I'm going to ask you to think about this: Why is poaching so much greater here in the Gardiner Basin than anywhere else in the state? That's a fact." He pauses to let that shocker sink in. "I would ask all of you in this room, on both sides of this issue, to look inside yourself and answer that question."

Shauna asks Sheppard, "Does that imply that tolerance is lower here or is that because we know our wolves and we know when they go missing?"

Sheppard nods his head thoughtfully, then divulges that he has lived and worked as a wildlife agent in other communities including McCall, Idaho (a state infamous for hunting and poaching wolves). He tells us that people in these other locales could not poach any wildlife without someone calling to tell him about it. But no one calls him to report poaching in Gardiner.

I don't want to believe that Gardiner residents permit more poaching. And I'm not alone. I can feel the discomfort in the room as Gardiner residents, both for and against wolves, try to digest our town's new title as Montana's top wolf-poaching area.

For a few more minutes, both sides comment, but somehow the fight has gone out of the room. Finally, Sheppard wraps up the meeting by saying that the public comment period will end soon. We can submit a written comment even if we spoke tonight.

As Leo, Mary, and I leave the warmth of the meeting room and step into the cool of the evening, we vow to submit written comments. We hope that the commissioners will cast their final vote in July as they did in May and keep the quota at two wolves. But who knows?

A few weeks later, I receive an email from Nathan, alerting Bear Creek Council members that MFWP biologists have read all the comments and submitted yet another proposal. This one recommends increasing the quota from two to four wolves in Unit 313. The commissioners will vote on the new proposal in three days. Nathan urges us to write the commissioners again and ask them to honor their original vote.

Staring at Nathan's email, I worry that the commissioners might accept the new proposal as a way of splitting the difference between those who want to save wolves and those who want to shoot wolves. I send an email to each of the commissioners, urging them to set the quota at two.

Locally, Nathan's alert generated a strong response. Not only did many Bear Creek Council members email the four commissioners, Ilona and Nathan called and spoke with some of them. Other conservation organizations rallied members too.

A few days later, I check my email and find one from Ilona with a subject line that proclaims: "FWP Commissioners Voted for 2 Wolf Quota in 313." I release a quiet howl of delight.

In the end, our teamwork paid off. Like the wolves we strive to protect, working as a pack is critical. I think about the valuable time and energy that so many people invested on behalf of wolves. Each pack member that showed up at a meeting made a difference. Each pack member's voice raised—whether in person, online, or by phone—made a difference.

Knowing that four wolves will live for another year, I'm thankful to be a member of this pack.

13

An Elk Encounter

——

Mary and I have planned a long weekend that we will spend without controversy. We will not attend any meetings, read any studies, or write any letters to government agencies about grizzlies, bison, wolves, or the gold mine that a greedy opportunist wants to dig on Yellowstone's border. We will not do anything that looks, sounds, or feels like advocacy.

We start our day by simply standing shoulder to shoulder at our large dining room window, mesmerized by the morning light painting Electric Peak in watercolors. Moments like this drew us here.

After a while, movement in the vacant lot across the street steals our attention from the peak. A female elk wanders into view, having climbed an animal trail that leads from the center of town, up a hillside, and into our neighborhood. She crosses the vacant lot, reaches the gravel street, begins walking past our house, and then stops and cranes her neck to look behind her.

Mary and I follow her gaze and watch with joyous surprise as a calf appears. The brown newborn with white spots wobbles on spindly legs. When the calf reaches the road, it manages an uncoordinated turn—maybe its first ever—and teeters toward mom. She walks back and licks the calf's head and body. When the cleaning is complete, the calf lays down on the sun-warmed gravel road. While the calf snoozes, mom stands guard, ripping and tearing at our neighbor's grass and flowers, famished after giving birth. Moments later the calf awakens and manages to stand on shaky legs. The pair continue their morning stroll down the road.

"Wow, that's beautiful," I say, awestruck.

"Yeah, I thought we'd have to go into the park to see the babies," Mary says. "Who would have thought they would come to us."

When we wintered at the Buffalo Ranch, we were on our way back to Oregon well before babies started popping out. When we considered moving here, spring's wild newborns were high on our must-see list. We found those newborn bison about a month ago and now here we stand in our home, basking in the glow of happiness and sunlight, watching this elk calf explore its world. The youngster lurches forward a few steps, lies down, arises, and wobbles ahead once again. The mom alternates her time between cleaning and grazing. We pinch ourselves to be certain we aren't dreaming, that this sighting—this gift—is real.

The mom and her calf disappear for the rest of the day, but the next morning they nestle beneath a tall but ravaged lilac bush in our next-door neighbor's front yard. And I mean ravaged. The lilac, old and unprotected by fencing, is a staple on the menu of our abundant neighborhood elk and mule deer. The only surviving leaves are those above the elk's reach. Elk stand as tall as horses and can reach high for a plant they enjoy. This spring we have watched elk stand on their rear legs, their front hooves dangling in the air, to gain an extra two feet of fresh green on this lilac and a golden willow in the same neighbor's back yard.

At the moment, mom and calf don't seem hungry. They stand and, now accompanied by another female, saunter across the street to the vacant lot, the calf sandwiched between the two adults. In just one day, the youngster's walk has become more confident and coordinated. Developing quickly is essential; the calf only has about two weeks to hide, nurse, and rest before it must be able to graze with the herd.

About an hour later, I'm back at the dining room window, again enjoying the view of Electric Peak and its lesser—but still dramatic—neighbor Sepulcher Mountain. With this view, I fear we may wear a bare spot in the wool rug beneath the window. When I pull my eyes away from the mountains and again look to the beat-up lilac, I spot a female elk bedded in the sparse shade at the base of the bush. Head high, ears alert, she looks up the road, past our house. I follow her attentive stare and see a woman jogging down the road in the direction of the elk. She's a tourist who has rented a house on this street for a few days. She has ear buds in and seems oblivious to the elk as she passes within six feet of it. Her nonchalance makes me nervous.

If the jogger was a local, she would probably have heard the buzz about the elk around here and probably be more attentive. Gardiner has its own online community bulletin board. People post all kinds of things, including warnings about wildlife. Just the other day, a woman reported that she and a friend were chased by a female elk despite keeping ample distance and a fenced playground between them and the animal. Her post corralled a herd of responses. Two locals who live near the sighting confirmed that the elk was chasing people because she had hidden her newborn nearby. Another person described how elk in his neighborhood have stashed their calves between outbuildings; in flower beds; and under porches, decks, and trucks. An old-timer said that in her twenty-two years here, this year is particularly heavy with elk protecting calves.

Some scientists have dubbed this behavior "human shielding." Elk know that mother and calf are vulnerable in the first few weeks after birth. Elk also know that wolves don't usually hunt in Gardiner. So some elk come here to give birth and keep their calves safe until the young can move with the herd and run from predators.

Thinking the jogger lucky to have not been charged by the elk, I move from the window to putter around the house. When the view from the window captures me again, I look up the road and there's the woman returning, jogging toward home. And there's the elk, standing beside the lilac and staring at the jogger. The woman, ear buds in, still does not appear to notice the elk.

When the jogger passes the lilac, the elk charges. The woman glances over her shoulder, spots the elk, screams, and sprints. The elk, taller and four times heavier, stays right behind the panting sprinter, though the animal could catch, pass, or run right over her. It's clear to me that the elk is not going to hurt the woman. Though the jogger—who glances back and shrieks again—thinks differently.

The woman sprints past our house and closes in on the finish line, the safety of her rental. She bangs through the gate of the chain link fence, bounds up the porch steps, and bends over with hands on hips like a runner who has just finished a fifty-yard dash. Which she has. When her companions rush from the house, encircle her, and ask what happened, I can hear parts of the loud explanation between her ragged sobs.

Meanwhile, the elk—not even breathing hard and wearing that look of disdain that female elk do so well—strolls past our house, into the vacant lot, down the hill, and out of sight. I stand there, relieved for the jogger and not believing what I have just seen. When I go to share the story with Mary, I find her at the window of the room she has converted to her music studio. Ukelele in hand, she sees me, shakes her head in dismay, and says that after she heard the first scream, she stopped playing and watched the race too.

A couple of hours later, I decide to go outside and tackle a minor repair on the cargo trailer we use to carry bicycles and sports gear. When I pop my head into the studio to tell Mary I'm going to the garage, she raises a pencil from the sheet of music she's working on and gives me a funny look.

"What?" I ask.

"Do you think that's a good idea with those elk around?"

"Oh," I scoff, "I'll just be right outside the garage."

Without a word, she gives me a smile that I like much less than her only-in-Yellowstone smile. This one says, *Don't say I didn't warn you.*

Before I turn to leave, I give her a look that says *I'll be darned if I'm going to let some elk keep me prisoner in my own house on such a fine spring day.* It was a long look.

But having been reminded of the screaming sprinter, I huff to the dining room window to see if the coast is clear. The only sign of elk is a female's head in the shade of a tree in the vacant lot across the street. I see no calf. Though I have read those community bulletin board warnings about elk mothers hiding their calves, for some reason I assume that the lone elk under the tree is the one from yesterday without a calf. She's not the problem; I should be safe. But just in case, I go out the back door and into the rear of the garage, keeping our nice solid house between me and any animal in the throes of postpartum aggression.

I gather the tools I need for the repair, walk to the overhead door, hit the wall-mounted button to open it, and wait as it rises. When it's open, I step from the shade of the garage into bright sunlight, squinting in the glare. I see that the elk across the road is now on her feet and staring at me. Her stance reminds me of the posturing yesterday, just before the elk chased the screamer. Ignoring what this may mean, I continue toward the trailer; I'm only six feet from the open door, for God's sake.

But those few extra feet must mean something to the elk, because here she comes, bounding across the road and into our driveway. I stop and stare at her, stunned. She does not stop. I throw my arms wide over my head and yell, "Stop!" Now, I know she doesn't understand English, but this is all I can muster at the moment. The elk skids to a noisy halt—legs locked, hooves sliding over concrete. Her flared nostrils are about four feet from the brim of the baseball cap atop my astonished head.

The elk stares at me, eyes wide, ears straight up. As I stare back, my hands still above my head, like a man being robbed, she conveys a clear, silent message: *What are you doing in my pasture, little man?*

"OK," I whisper, "just stay right there. I don't need to work on that trailer today."

The elk exhales loudly through her long nose, lowers her head, and then raises it. Did she just nod "OK"?

"All right, lady, I'm going to back into the garage. You can have the driveway."

Another noisy exhale.

Watching for any movement from her, I take one step back. No change. I take another step and gauge from the corner of my eye that the next will put me in the garage. I drift to my right, toward the button that will close the overhead door. The elk drops her head and takes a step forward.

"No way!" I shout. "You're not coming in here with me."

She stops and raises her head. I take another step back. This one puts me just inside the garage, and my right hand slaps that button like someone trying to break the glass cover on a fire alarm. The motor hums. The door squeals as it moves in its track. The elk takes one step back. As the door descends between us, I drop to hands and knees so that I can keep an eye on her. With the door just a foot away from closing, I see her hooves turn and move out of my limited sight. The door meets the concrete and clunks to a stop. In the dark silence, my shaky sigh of relief resounds. I look around, wondering if this really happened. Was I just bluff charged by an elk in my driveway? What in the heck have we gotten ourselves into by moving here?

That trailer repair can wait. I throw the tools on the workbench and retreat out the back door. Now I have to go in, face the music, and admit to Mary that she was right... again.

14

Fawns and Finances

———

Mary and I are back on Old Yellowstone Trail, that dirt road that runs through the Gardiner Basin and past the Stephens Creek Capture Facility. But this time we're not using binoculars to count the number of bison that might be captured by the Park Service or wasted by shooters. That sad and controversial process is over—for this year. Now it's early June, and we are here for a happier reason: our first mountain bike ride of spring. We hope to be lucky enough to see more babies in the wild. Though I would prefer not to have another run-in with a protective mother.

The road is free of traffic so we can ride beside one another. We pedal away from the Roosevelt Arch and soon pass the entrance road that climbs to the Gardiner cemetery with its 192 graves, some dating back as early as the 1880s. As we pedal leisurely, we talk about how we enjoy late spring in the northern Rockies. Today is what locals call a bluebird day, the sun bright in a cloudless sky the color of the mountain bluebirds that have recently returned. The morning is balmy; we don't need jackets.

As we cycle through the ups and downs of rumpled hills, our breathing increases and chatting decreases. We stop and dismount to catch our breath and take in the view before the road descends to the basin floor. The scene today is quite different from that of February. The basin glows with a vivid green instead of dull winter browns and whites. The Yellowstone River, flecked with whitewater, flows high and fast with snowmelt. Electric Peak still dominates, but its glacier-carved flank is now only half-covered with snow.

We climb back on our bikes and enjoy the rush of the downhill speed and flow of the curves that lead to the basin floor. Once on the flat, the ride slows and the road doglegs to the right and left. As we enter the second dogleg, Mary, close beside me, whispers, "Hey, look, two female pronghorn. Let's stop and check them out. "

We pull over and stand silent. The two pronghorn watching us are about as tall as deer but weigh less. Their bodies are white underneath and reddish-tan on the back. Their rumps are white.

"They both have swollen teats," I whisper to Mary, pleased that I noticed first.

She looks at me, nods her head, and silently mouths, *Good eyes*. Then she asks, "Where are the fawns? They must have stashed them somewhere."

We scan the knee-high sagebrush and rabbitbrush. After a fruitless search, we give up and return to watching the pair as they watch us. When they return to feeding, we mount up and ride away.

As we bounce through a washboard section of road, Mary, now ahead of me, rubbernecks to her left. She stops the bike, slides off the seat, and stands with feet planted beside the pedals. When I pull up beside her, she grins, points to her left, and whispers, "Babies!"

Now it's my turn to mime the silent Good Eyes award. I spot the four reddish-brown pronghorn fawns resting about thirty-five yards away. All four have seen us. One stands on wobbly legs; the others stay put, their heads just visible above the grass.

"We would have zoomed right by them if we had been in a car," I whisper. "I'll bet you these are the fawns of the mothers we just saw."

Since pronghorns usually give birth to two fawns each, we have stumbled upon what is called a nursery group. Two mothers have hidden their fawns together and gone off to graze. These fawns will spend the first three weeks of their lives like this. They will see their mothers only every three to four hours when the adults return to nurse, groom, and lead them to water. The rest of the time the babies remain hidden from the bobcats, wolves, bears, golden eagles, and especially coyotes that hunger for a taste of tender fawn.

"What's he doing here?" Mary asks. I look in the direction she indicates with the thrust of her chin and see an adult pronghorn standing some yards away from the fawns. A black patch on his cheek and twelve-inch-high pronged horns reveal he's a buck. He too studies us.

"Huh, that's a darn good question," I say. "Is he guarding the nursery? Or is he just an older solitary male who has stumbled upon the fawns like we did?"

We stand astride our bikes, considering another of Yellowstone's mysteries and captivated by the fawns' dark eyes, so gentle, so inviting, and so good at spotting predators. Those eyes, large in diameter and set on the sides of the head, provide a wide field of vision, enabling a pronghorn to catch sight of a predator from almost any direction.

Superb vision is just one of the adaptations of this species over the last twenty million years of evolving in North America. Compared to its body size, a pronghorn's windpipe, lungs, and heart are oversized and enable the animal to inhale and use lots of air. Each leg has two cushioned toes that act as shock absorbers. Add to this their light bone structure, and you've got a body built to sprint at forty-five to fifty miles per hour—that's faster than any predator they'll face today. Such speed was a lifesaver long ago when these fawns' ancestors had to outrun a now-extinct American cheetah.

Though pronghorn outlasted that cheetah, they have not fared so well with humans. When Euro-Americans arrived in the West, pronghorn were as abundant as bison—thirty-five million grazed the countryside, according to the NPS. Now, only about 500,000 survive, most in Montana and Wyoming.

For Yellowstone's pronghorn, the decline began in 1871 when homesteaders laid claim to this basin. Within thirty years, much of the vegetation that pronghorn depend upon—sagebrush, rabbitbrush, and wildflowers—had been removed by settlers determined to plow, plant, and harvest crops in this high desert. While the settlers grew non-native plants such as alfalfa and oats, pronghorn went in search of native plants. Those that remained were either shot by hunters or killed by ranchers who saw them as stealing food from their cattle. By the early 1900s the Park Service was in on the action, culling—killing—pronghorn because park management feared overgrazing.

By the 1930s, the prospects for pronghorn improved—as did the prospects for local ranchers, suffering agriculturally from a drought and strapped financially by the Great Depression. Congress, according to historian Aubrey Haines, authorized the purchase of 7,600 acres of land in Gardiner Basin to expand Yellowstone's northern boundary and provide more winter range for pronghorn. Great idea, but there was no federal money to do the buying. After a game preservation company in New York donated $14,000 (equivalent to $195,000 today), the park began acquiring. The ranchers took the money and moved away, but their non-native vegetation did not go with them. Even today, the remains of plantings by early settlers reduce the amount of native vegetation available to pronghorn.

Years of ranching and hunting and culling reduced Yellowstone's pronghorn herd from roughly 1,000 animals to the meager 450 left today. With such a small number remaining, the Park Service now calls pronghorn a species of special concern. They warn that Yellowstone's herd could be wiped out by disease or a severe winter.

Even without a natural disaster, two of the four fawns watching Mary and me will not see their first birthday. They will be lost to predators or disease. The two survivors will grow up feeling the crunch from development north of the park. Fences enclosing private land in Paradise Valley can block access to vital winter grazing when Yellowstone Park is covered in snow or ice.

The fawns have settled back into the high grass, heads down, only the pointed tips of their long ears showing. Thankful for sighting these wild babies, we mount up and pedal away.

A couple of miles later, we cycle past evidence of the financial wrangling that has given additional land to those fawns and other park wildlife. On either side of the road stand fence posts with no wires strung between them, nothing to get in the way of grazers. Removing the wires is a lifesaver for pronghorn. Though pronghorn can outrun predators, they cannot leap a fence like deer or elk. Pronghorn must crawl under the fencing, and when they do they are vulnerable.

Some of the fence posts bear a small yellow No Trespassing sign placed there by the Royal Teton Ranch, a spread owned by the Church Universal and Triumphant (CUT), the organization from which this additional grazing land came. The CUT bought its first property here in 1981 and had a rough start with the park and its other neighbors. As Scott McMillion reported in the Bozeman Daily Chronicle, "... church leaders butted heads with environmental groups, politicians, anti-cult groups, state regulators and officials from Yellowstone National Park, which was next door to the church's 12,000-acre Royal Teton Ranch. There were lawsuits with county, state and federal governments. Church officials were arrested on weapons charges."

But times and relationships change. In August of 1999 politicians and representatives from the CUT, environmental groups, and the Park Service came together in a meadow along Old Yellowstone Trail, near the place Mary and I are cycling. They celebrated the exchange of 6,300 acres of church land and a conservation easement on another 1,500 acres for $13 million in federal money. This wasn't altruism; the CUT had fallen on hard times and needed money— just like those Depression-era ranchers who sold out to the federal government in the 1930s.

Of course, those four fawns and their mothers, the rest of the pronghorn, all the deer, elk, bighorn sheep, and bison that depend on this basin don't care why the land went from private to public or why fencing was removed. They don't know about the backroom deals and millions of dollars spent to make this land available. They are more concerned with surviving harsh winters until spring returns, when the weather warms, food abounds, and life is good for them— and for two cyclists overjoyed to be their neighbors.

15

About Time

——

An artist's palette of blooming wildflowers and an ensemble of singing birds greet us as we start down the trail toward the valley cut eons ago by the Yellowstone River and Hellroaring Creek. While Mary and I have spent many hours during the winter on the roadside high above this valley, searching with spotting scopes for wolves on its snow-covered floor, we haven't hiked in for ten years.

As excitement and gravity propel us down the trail through several switchbacks, the delightful scent of June flowers arrives on an upslope breeze. We stop and I take in the beauty all around me. Mary identifies the flowers: arrowleaf balsam root and larkspur, wild strawberry and wild geranium, Rocky Mountain phlox and forget-me-nots.

As we navigate more switchbacks, a man and a woman approach, striding uphill at a fast clip, despite lugging full packs. When they pass, I notice that the man also carries an infant on his back. A few moments later another couple hauling packs and an infant go by. I admire the dedication of these parents to share this natural wonder with their offspring. I can't help but wonder about the relationship those infants—members of the next generation that will protect and care for Yellowstone—are developing with nature in general and this park in particular.

I recently met a few members of that next generation when I did a series of book signings at visitor centers within Yellowstone. Sitting at my table, a stack of books and a pen before me, I grew excited when the occasional teen or pre-teen approached and shared his or her dream to be a park ranger, a zoologist, or—in the case of one twelve-year-old girl—an ecologist. When I asked why she chose that job, she replied without hesitation, "Because I love animals, and I want to save the habitat they depend on." I shoved my chair back, stood up, and shook her hand. Then I shook the hand of her beaming mother. I thanked the mom for her part in instilling such environmental awareness, and I wished the young lady all the best in reaching her career goal. I told her that she gives me hope for the preservation of treasures like Yellowstone, in need of protection by her generation—in need of protection by every generation.

Mary and I leave the sun-warmed switchbacks and slip into the cool shade of conifers. We rest on a log and refresh in the moist hideaway. Mushrooms the color and size of small pancakes sprout among downed timber. What a luxury to have the time to sit and watch these mushrooms in our first Yellowstone spring.

When we long for sun, we move on. Soon we catch a whiff of sulfur, a timeless Yellowstone scent, drifting up from a riverside thermal area. We arrive at a suspension footbridge, as wide as a city sidewalk, thirty yards long, strung high above the Yellowstone River. We stop in the middle, lean against the railing, peer down, and stand in awe of the snow-melt-filled Yellowstone—the longest free-flowing river in the Lower 48—as it roars and foams and smashes its way along the rocky channel, taking with it the last of winter.

Crossing the footbridge, we continue downhill through dark forests and bright clearings until the trail delivers us to the valley floor, a wide-open expanse that charms with its subtle splendor of the diverse greens of grass, sage, and reeds. I take in the view and lose myself in the span of this valley. And in the time it spans. The boulders scattered around us and the reed-encircled pond that we are heading towards are evidence of glaciers moving through here some 15,000 years ago. Then there is 8,358-foot-high Hellroaring Mountain, on the opposite side of the Yellowstone River. Geologists estimate that this uplifted, triangular chunk of what they call basement rock—the foundation that creates the crust of this continent—formed almost three *billion* years ago. The closer, lower hills are remnants of volcanic eruptions and *only* fifty million years old, geologic infants.

Try as I might, I can't grasp the scope of these stretches of time. In truth, I struggle with the recognition that I have been walking this earth for more than six decades. Geologically, that's less than a fraction of an eye blink. But for me, a very long time and much too close to the end.

The sound of a coyote singing nearby brings me back to the present. Mary and I scan left and right but don't find the singer. The animal could be ten feet away and out of sight in the sage and grass that grows higher than a coyote stands tall.

We follow a little-used trail, and when we reach that glacier-created pond, we pause to listen to a yellow-headed blackbird's solo in the tall reeds. While the Audubon guide claims that this song, "a hoarse, harsh, scraping," may be the worst of any North American bird, I don't find it so. I smile every time I hear it. Scientists have unearthed 100,000-year-old yellow-headed blackbird fossils in the American Southwest. These birds have been singing from reeds for far longer than we have been eradicating wildlife on this continent one endangered species at a time.

From the corner of my eye, I catch the brown flash of a Uinta ground squirrel, all eight ounces of it, scampering from the pond's edge to the cover of some nearby rocks. Now there's a creature that counts its time above ground in days. Each year only about a hundred days may pass between its emergence from hibernation in April and return underground as early as mid-July.

We leave the pond and, crossing the verdant valley, make our way toward the distant clamor of Hellroaring Creek. At the designated ford, whitewater crashes from bank to bank. We hear the sharp rumble of an unseen boulder, dislodged underwater and rolled along by the torrent, crashing into other rocks in its path. It will be weeks before anyone can safely ford this creek impersonating a river.

That's no problem for us, we hadn't planned on crossing. We turn and stroll upstream along the creek, seeking just the right spot for lunch before we must climb all those switchbacks out of here. Finding an inviting bank covered in soft grass, we stop, wiggle out of our daypacks, and start to settle in. Just as I rest my head on my pack and pull my hat over my eyes, Mary kicks the bottom of my foot and whispers, "Uh-oh, look at that."

I sit up, turn to where she's pointing, and find a bull bison, ten yards away and plodding toward us. He wears his springtime outfit, with more than half of his winter coat now shed. Sun reflects where his now fur-free hide is as smooth as leather. Sun highlights the amber and orange of the thick brown winter fur that still hangs on. Though his head is down, and he doesn't seem to have noticed us, he is too close. We stand, throw our packs on, and scamper upstream in the shallows along the edge of Hellroaring Creek, sometimes boulder hopping, sometimes splashing through quiet eddies.

When we squish back onto the bank, the bison has stopped, raised his massive head, and is staring at us. I zero in on his tail. Though a bison is not an expressive animal—it can't, for example, smile like a dog—that tail tells us all we need to know, just as it did when we watched the Mollie's sort and sift a bison herd. It's well below half-mast. Our sudden appearance hasn't stressed him too much.

Still, Mary and I keep our eyes on that tail as we hasten upstream along the bank, aiming to put at least the twenty-five yards the Park Service requires between us and the bull. The bison adds to that buffer by turning his tail toward us and grazing downstream.

As the distance increases, we agree it's safe to proceed with the picnic. We claim another spot, and as we relax onto the sloping bank amidst grass and flowers, rocks and sunshine, Mary says, "That was eye-opening." I nod, and she adds, "That could have just as easily been a grizzly."

So right. They are all out of their dens. Now is their time for another season of park-wide wandering, putting on pounds in preparation for the next big sleep. I wouldn't want to surprise a grizzly like we surprised that bison.

I look at Mary, pull my sunglasses down to the tip of my nose, and say, "I'll watch your back, if you watch mine."

As we sit back-to-back beside Hellroaring Creek, scanning for bison or bears and rejoicing in the creek's sound and power, I'm elated that we moved next door to this paradise. I don't know how much time I have left above ground. Don't know how much longer I will be able to walk or bicycle or ski into this wild majesty. But however many days, weeks, months, or years I have, Yellowstone is where I want to spend them.

Summer

16

Swarmed by the Faithful

———

In July, in the hectic crush of Yellowstone's tourist season, I am spending four full days in the Old Faithful area. Without a car. Happily stranded. I am staying in a room in the Old Faithful Inn. Not just any room, but one that was once the office of Robert Reamer, the architect who designed the Inn and a number of other buildings in Yellowstone and Gardiner. From this third-floor room, I see a busy parking lot, some of the Upper Geyser Basin's steaming geysers and colorful hot springs, and the surrounding lodgepole pine-covered hills.

I try to avoid Old Faithful in summer, but Mary's duties as a volunteer have brought us here; I am the tagalong husband. The two of us drove from Gardiner in an otherwise empty fourteen-passenger Yellowstone Forever bus. Mary is now out driving that bus filled with participants and their artist-instructor, all in attendance for a field seminar. For the next four days, Mary will drive her passengers to places where the instructor expects the landscape and light will make for satisfying drawings and paintings.

While Mary's schedule is fixed, mine is wide open. Each morning before she and the crowds of tourists are up, I walk the boardwalk in the Upper Geyser Basin for a couple of hours. I wait for the sun to rise over the hill and then watch in awe as first light blesses the basin. Each evening, before Mary returns, I walk again as the show ends, the sun sets, and—I can't believe my luck—a full moon shines.

In between the sun and moon rising, I retreat—as I am doing now—to Reamer's office and hide from the hordes. I sit on a wood-and-wicker straight-backed chair at an old copper-topped table and write, scribbling on paper, pecking on a laptop. I hope to tap into some of Reamer's creativity, evidenced in this building that is now a National Historic Landmark.

Throughout these days of craving creativity, I periodically lift my head from writing and gaze out the window. I watch clouds come. I watch clouds go. I feel soothing sulfur-scented breezes on my face. I listen to the frenzy of diesel tour buses arriving and emptying or filling and departing. I hear the patter of bus drivers and guides, the crying of babies, the barking of dogs, the rumbling of motorcycles. And about every ninety minutes, I grin at the laughter and applause, the whoops and hollers as Old Faithful, true to its name, erupts, bringing joy to those congregated on the Inn's nearby balcony, positioned so perfectly by Reamer.

But summer is not my favorite time to geyser gaze. I prefer winter, pre-dawn, minus twenty degrees, snow falling. That usually thins the crowd to just Mary and me, as it did a few months ago when we climbed through the snow-flocked forest to Observation Point, visible from Reamer's office as a small, distant opening in the pines across the Upper Geyser Basin. I keep a favorite photograph from that trip: Mary, in profile, bundled up for winter, sitting alone on one of the many snow-covered benches surrounding Old Faithful, patiently awaiting an eruption. Not another soul in sight.

But one summer, a few years ago, at the height of tourist season, I couldn't resist the lure of watching Old Faithful from within a swarm of strangers...

I stood in the crowded lobby of the Old Faithful Lodge and stared at a large sign on the wall that resembled the "Will Return At" sign on a closed mom-and-pop store. It informed me that Old Faithful's next eruption would return in forty-five minutes. I pushed one of the lobby's massive double doors open and stepped outside onto a concrete sidewalk wider than a two-car driveway. I strolled to the expansive viewing area, curving halfway around Old Faithful. A sign described the viewing areas here and in other sections of the park as constructed of lumber that recycled the equivalent of about three million plastic bottles. Impressed with that effort, I settled onto a shiny, smooth, gray, plastic-lumber bench.

Wisps of steam rose into the air from Old Faithful's cone and gave the only hint of the eruption, now a half-hour away. Hundreds of feet from me, at the other end of the benches, two people sat. Just three of us in a viewing area that would soon hold a couple-thousand seated and standing seekers. For most of them, catching Old Faithful's eruption makes their trip to Yellowstone official, like having a passport stamped upon entering a foreign country.

Old Faithful has been faithful since at least 1870, when the Washburn Expedition stayed here for twenty-four hours. While that may seem short, it's longer than most tourists stay now. Like today's throngs, General Washburn and his men had other sights to see. Unlike today, they did not have benches made of plastic lumber. During their visit to the Upper Geyser Basin, the geyser erupted often enough to merit the name Old Faithful. Over the intervening years, the Park Service has collected data and devised a formula that faithfully predicts the eruption within ten minutes.

The eruption we awaited had its origins tens of thousands of years ago in the snow and rain that fell on porous hills around the basin. Countless drops of moisture penetrated the ground and its millions of cracks and fissures, beginning a slow journey toward the center of the Earth. They trickled and flowed toward the molten magma that in Yellowstone is unusually close to the Earth's surface. That cold snow and cool rain eventually collected into a large heated chamber somewhere below the spot where we sat.

I glanced at my watch; we had twenty minutes until the predicted (not scheduled, mind you) eruption. All the front row seats were taken as were many in the second row. Some people sat on the edge of the boardwalk, seeking a better photo opportunity. As they killed time, they shuffled their feet, scarring the delicate layer of sparkling white sinter deposited by countless Old Faithful eruptions.

A husband and wife sat near me. She said, "We've got twenty minutes to wait." He replied, "I can stand ten." I watched as three camera-carrying tourists ignored the numerous and obvious "Do Not Leave the Trail" signs and entered a closed area near the geyser. While this is not as bad as when tourists in the 1880s broke off chunks of Old Faithful's cone as souvenirs, it still serves to remind that we can love this geyser, this basin, this park to death.

As I sat there, the geyser continued to hint at its next display by occasionally bubbling forth water. That water is just the top of a very tall, thin column rising from that subterranean heating chamber. The Park Service knows the column is thin because some years ago scientists lowered a camera into Old Faithful and discovered the outlet tube constricts to just four inches across, about the diameter of a dessert plate.

This constriction and the column of water above and below it cork the outlet of the subterranean chamber, turning it into a pressure cooker. Under great pressure, the trapped water rises in temperature well past boiling point. But the water does not boil. Instead, the superheated liquid expands, exerting force on the column, causing some water to bubble out from the geyser.

That escaping water, at five predicted minutes from blast-off, heightened my excitement and that of the tourists around me, who by now had filled all available seats and most standing room. But a young woman on my right groused, "I don't have five minutes to wait." Her male partner cooed, "Oh yes you do." She snapped back, "How would you know?" To my left, a dad, glancing again and again at his large, silver wristwatch, told his flock of spouse and children, "We have to get to the Tetons by dinner."

When did this marvel of nature become just another stop along the vacation highway, a wonder to bag in our rush to the next must-see?

Not all present were so time-obsessed. A lone bull bison grazed about twenty yards away, between the crowd and Old Faithful. After the first bubbling tease of the geyser, he walked toward the middle of the seating area. Perhaps he sensed the upcoming eruption. Perhaps he didn't like people watching him eat. Whatever his reason, he was just five feet from and heading directly for the plastic boardwalk jammed with people. As he walked toward them, the tourists just stood there as if watching a movie. Hundreds of cameras beeped and clicked and whirred, capturing his light-footed progress.

I watched with dread as a man holding an infant in one hand and a camera in the other jostled *toward* the oncoming bison. This reminded me of a film I had seen at the Mammoth Hot Springs Visitor Center. In footage from a home movie, a family parked their car and walked too close to a lone bison. Without warning, the bull charged, knocking down the teenage brother and sister. The brother scrambled to his feet and fled. The bison head-butted the sister around like a soccer ball. Though she was not seriously injured, the image stayed with me. That film—or one like it—should be required viewing for every visitor, especially that baby-toting fool and the crowd around him who were finally—grudgingly—making a ten-foot wide path for the largest land mammal in North America, a wild, unpredictable, one-ton creature with sharp horns.

As the bison tip-toed across the boardwalk and the crowd rushed to get a better view spot in his wake, Old Faithful continued bubbling and teasing. Each tease reduced the pressure in the chamber below. After enough teasing, the pressure dropped to a point where the chamber's water could flash to steam. Steam fills more space than water, and this tremendous expansion forced the remaining water out of the underground chamber, up the column, through that four-inch constriction, and into the blue, cloudless Yellowstone sky. Eruption!

The crowd clapped and oohed and aahed as about 8,000 gallons of water accompanied by hissing steam gushed thirteen stories above our upturned, smiling faces.

To my left, the Teton-obsessed dad clicked his camera once and barked to his family, "OK, I've got it. Let's go!"

Within thirty seconds of the first tall gush, people began their escape. Within a minute, the exodus toward surrounding eateries was in full swing. (When Mary and I worked at one of those concessions years ago, these faithful onslaughts of hungry tourists were called "geyser rushes.") By the time Old Faithful had completed its three and one-half minute spectacle, the viewing area was almost empty. And the exits from the surrounding parking lots were gridlocked.

As the swarm of strangers receded, I remained seated, eyes on the sky. I inhaled a final whiff of sulfur. The lingering drops from the eruption caressed my face. I sat in awe of this water that first fell from the sky millennia ago, traveled deep below our feet, became superheated, flashed into steam, and finally gushed to glory as Old Faithful.

17

Wolves and Ravens

———

Many years ago, when I first visited Yellowstone, I was awed by its grandeur: massive mountains, rushing rivers, colorful thermal features, and abundant wildlife. But as I have since immersed myself in the park, I have learned that grandeur also reveals itself in subtle and surprising ways. One of those is the incredible connection between wolves and ravens.

Mary and I have spent many days in the park seeking or watching wolves. That translates into many hours looking for ravens that can lead us to wolves or observing ravens on wolf kills. While this connection between these two species is obvious, I have often wondered just how deep the connection goes.

Shauna Baron, our friend and an instructor for Yellowstone Forever, knows ravens and wolves. Originally from New York, she worked at a wolf sanctuary in Colorado and landed in Yellowstone not long after the first wolves returned in 1995. She has spent two fulfilling decades in the park as an instructor and guide. That translates into countless hours spent enthralled by the intelligence and antics of ravens, especially as they interact with wolves. Today, Baron is speaking with a group of park visitors about ravens and wolves, and I have the chance to listen in, like a fly on the wall.

Just moments into her talk, Baron recalls how she once laughed at a Yellowstone raven and wolf pup playing. The raven teased the pup and then hopped away. "I was amazed," Baron says, "to see the pup catch the bird, and the bird roll on its back and let the puppy climb on top of it. The raven imitated a puppy's movements, chewed on the pup's muzzle gently. And the pup chewed on the bird's beak."

Though she only witnessed this mimicking behavior once, she has often delighted in ravens and pups playing other games. They'll play fetch; a raven tosses a stick that the wolf chases. They'll play tug of war; a raven holds a stick in its beak, while the pup bites the other end and pulls.

Ravens especially enjoy yearling wolves, Baron says. She has watched a raven throw a pine cone down a snow-covered slope "and the yearling will go sledding down the hill to get it. But the raven usually beats the wolf, brings the pine cone back to the top of the hill, and they play again." Such interactive play, she believes, cements the future connection between the two species. "Often as that puppy grows up what we'll see is that the bond is really strong in some wolves, and they'll play with ravens even as adults."

Baron's field observations and opinions on ravens presented today are consistent with the results of research conducted by the well-respected scientist, Bernd Heinrich. He has studied ravens for decades. He wrote the ultimate resource on this bird, *Mind of the Raven*. I've spent hours reading and highlighting in his book.

Heinrich visited Yellowstone shortly after wolves were reintroduced. He and Baron probably passed each other on the two-lane road through the Lamar Valley. In *Mind of the Raven*, Heinrich makes the distinction that Yellowstone's wolves *interested* him, but the park's ravens *intrigued* him. He watched the birds every day, noting subtle differences between ravens in the West and those he knew well from his years of research in the East. He even heard four raven calls in Yellowstone that were new to him. At wolf kills in the park, Heinrich saw how ravens "always arrive immediately and start feeding at each fresh carcass. Ravens often arrive before the elk is down."

On one outing, Heinrich left the park through the north entrance at Gardiner and hiked into the bordering national forest, just above where Mary and I now live. Elk hunting season was booming, and he found sixteen gut piles, elk innards left by human hunters. None of the piles had ravens feeding on them. This surprised him. Why would ravens reject such a bounty?

Returning to the park, Heinrich drove east through the Lamar Valley, keeping a sharp eye out along the way. He detected a pattern: ravens only fed where wolves were dining. "With wolves present, the ravens had no fear of the carcass. They could go in and get their own meat." He speculated that perhaps ravens, after evolving with wolves over millions of years, were simply most comfortable when wolves were around

When Heinrich talked with Yellowstone wolf researchers, he discovered that many took for granted the connection between wolves and ravens. He convinced them to dig deeper, to try to understand how and why the animals have developed this relationship. By the next winter, one of the researchers, Dan Stahler, began gathering data on park ravens. After reviewing Stahler's early data, Heinrich wrote, "It is beginning to look as if ravens are dependent on wolves not only to kill for them and to open carcasses, but also to overcome their innate shyness of large food, whether in the form of a carcass or a pile."

I wonder if the ravens' need to have wolves around before eating large food sources has changed in the twenty years since Heinrich spotted those raven-free gut piles in the national forest. Mary and I often walk for exercise along a road during hunting season in that same national forest. We see elk gut piles—and now bison gut piles too. Hordes of ravens darken the sky and smother the gut piles. But we see no wolves, Perhaps wolves have christened the piles earlier. Or perhaps after years with wolves back in Yellowstone, the ravens feel safe without wolves present.

We hear more of Stahler's findings when Baron tells her group that ravens arrive within one minute of wolves making a kill, with an average of twenty-eight ravens at each carcass. She estimates a raven can consume only about two-thirds of a pound of meat at one time. "Once their crop is full," she says, "they just start caching food, flying back and forth and hiding stuff all over the place. And they can remember thousands of locations, so they've always got something available." One beakful at a time adds up: she has calculated that a flock—also called a conspiracy—of ravens can whisk away more than 300 pounds of meat from a carcass by the end of a busy day. The conspirators "outcompete the wolves for the majority of the meat," she adds, shaking her head in wonder.

"Cache while it lasts and eat later," is raven policy, according to Heinrich. He once observed forty ravens at a carcass and estimated that together they may have made more than 4,000 caches in a single day. He found that ravens "in crowds in the field almost always cache food very far from where they get it." And no two caches are in the same place.

Curious as to how ravens find such widely scattered caches, Heinrich conducted an experiment with fifteen wild-caught ravens. He found that the "birds easily remembered caches made a day or two before. They had poor ability to remember caches made two weeks earlier, and they were virtually unable to recover month-old caches." He concluded that the minds of ravens are like a chalkboard on which they register many cache locations. After each retrieval, they "erase" that cache from the chalkboard. His experiments with caching ravens revealed to him "more flexibility than had ever been observed in any other animal."

But the raven's flexibility would be worthless without flexible wolves. "It's rare," Baron tells her group, "that wolves kill ravens, but they chase them off all the time. They'll kill eagles; they'll kill magpies; they'll definitely kill coyotes. But I have only seen or heard of wolves killing ravens maybe a half a dozen times in twenty years." And a wolf that kills a raven pays a price. "All the other ravens will mob that wolf and just pummel it, like 'you killed my friend.'" She has also observed ravens in what seems to be mourning. "The other ravens surround their dead comrade and chase everything off of it. There is a definite understanding that something bad just happened."

This peaceful coexistence between wolves and ravens fostered the growth of Yellowstone's raven population. Baron dips again into Stahler's research when she tells her group that before wolves were reintroduced there were only 60 to 120 ravens in all of Yellowstone's Northern Range and just thirty to fifty in another part of the park. But, Baron says, within a year or two of wolves' return, observers counted up to 137 ravens on a single carcass.

Wolves have learned to compensate for the ever-present and always hungry ravens. "You really only need four individual wolves to be successful hunting elk," Baron explains. "But wolves will often tolerate large numbers in their pack." One theory is that a pack with more wolves can consume more of the kill before ravens airlift it away.

While wolf packs chase ravens away, some individual wolves may willingly share their bounty. "Ravens," Baron explains, "are so intelligent that they can identify individual wolves, just like you and I can. And they learn very quickly which wolves will tolerate them more than others. Throughout a pup's life, the ravens are conditioning them to their presence."

Her observations of raven behavior lead Baron to conclude with obvious admiration: "Ravens are one of the smartest birds on Earth. If they see you do something, they can mimic you. And they're really good at solving problems."

Heinrich's research supports Baron's observations. He calculated that the brains of ravens are larger compared to their body size than the brains of any other bird. He tested to see how well ravens can use that relatively big brain. Could ravens evaluate choices to make an intelligent decision without first trying each choice? His test involved hanging from a branch a long string with a piece of meat tied to it. He devised the test so that a raven could only get the prize by sitting on the branch and pulling up the string. That would require taking *at least ten distinct steps in a precise order.*

The ravens excelled, completing the pull-up in as little as thirty seconds after first touching the string. What's more, the birds who pulled the meat up never tried to fly off with it still tied to the string. Each seemed to know that the tethered meat would be ripped from their beak in flight. To Heinrich, they appeared to have figured this out in their heads without being jerked around by painful trial and error.

After more experiments, Heinrich concluded that ravens "…experience some level of consciousness, and use it for insight to make decisions. Whether that is 'intelligence' is subjective, but according to most people it is." After watching ravens prosper by stealing from wolves, I believe the birds possess exceptional intelligence.

Baron has marveled at the practical side of raven intelligence, which allows the birds to find food even without the aid of wolves. She has watched ravens break into the packs of snowmobilers in Yellowstone parking lots. "Ravens can open zippers, Velcro, buttons, and flaps. If there is food just inside a window, they'll tear through the screen."

The group laughs when Baron tells them she has seen ravens open jars, cooperatively and singly. She describes two ravens in a parking lot with a peanut butter jar between them. "One bird was holding onto the bottom of the jar with its feet, and the other bird was on the opposite end twisting the lid with its feet." Another time she watched a determined lone raven open a jar by holding it with one foot, pecking at the lid in the correct direction, and "spinning the lid off, just tap, tap, tap."

Experienced storyteller that she is, Baron saves the best for last, ending her talk with a favorite anecdote that highlights the strength of the wolf-raven connection. One winter day she watched an adult male wolf navigate across a frozen lake with a raven flying low overhead. The bird landed on the ice in front of the wolf.

"The wolf," Baron says, "did a play bow, head down, butt in the air, tail wagging as if to say, 'Let's play!'" The raven then flew to the edge of the lake, grabbed a piece of rye grass, and came back onto the ice, grass in tow. The bird sat with the big blade of grass in its mouth as if tempting the wolf. The wolf crouched down, preparing to leap toward the bird. When the wolf leapt, the bird opened its mouth and let the wind send the blade of grass flying. The wolf did "a Scooby-Doo routine slipping and sliding all over the ice" as it tried to catch the airborne grass. "But the bird beat him to it and sat on the ice holding the blade of grass, teasing the wolf again." The two played like this for seven minutes before the wolf continued across the frozen lake.

In a harsh winter world where survival is a daily challenge for both animals, those seven minutes of play speak volumes about the amazing relationship between wolves and ravens. After observing ravens, listening to Shauna Baron, and reading Bernd Heinrich, I realize that connection—that subtle grandeur—is greater than I ever imagined.

18

Passages

———

Mary, Leo, Karen, and I leave the bunkhouse of the Lamar Buffalo Ranch and start hiking toward a particular knob a couple of miles to the west. The side of that knob is covered with tall grasses, golden in August. The top—a little over 8,000-feet high—is dark green under a cover of whitebark pine.

The knob differs little from others around it, except in Karen's mind and heart. That place is her refuge, a secluded spot where she sometimes sought solace when she worked eight busy summers at the ranch. She will soon finish her last summer—presumably, the place is hard to leave. Since we've spent time together at the ranch and meandering in the Lamar Valley, she invited us meanderthals to join her as she says goodbye to this passage in her life and this place.

Karen leads the way as we rock-hop across the middle fork of Rose Creek, jump across the west fork, and stop. We turn our faces toward the sun, now rising behind nearby Druid Peak. The morning light plays over Specimen Ridge and the Lamar Valley.

Leaving the creek behind, we start climbing Ranger Hill, a ridge that rises near the ranch. During the first winter we spent here, we sometimes watched the Lamar Canyon pack rest on the slope of Ranger Hill, gleaning warmth from the morning sun. Climbing, we follow a narrow animal trail through the grasses that adorn the hillside. We come upon a bull bison resting, blocking the trail. We make a wide and silent detour around him. His old eyes follow us, but he makes no effort to stand.

Further down the trail, Leo and I stop to admire the long morning shadows on Druid Peak. While Mary and Karen continue the hike, Leo points to a distant ridge and says that's where he imagines wolf 10M howling, pleading with his mate to leave the Rose Creek acclimation pen in the winter of 1995.

That pen still stands; it's about a mile from here and hidden from view on a forested slope. It was one of the first enclosures built for the controversial release of wolves into Yellowstone. Three wolves, 10M, the alpha male; 9F, the alpha female; and 7F, a pup, were carted from Canada and placed in the pen so that they could acclimate to Yellowstone—and not feel compelled to run back to Canada once released.

Armed guards protected the pen and the wolves from afar, since death threats had been made against the captive animals. One winter, I snowshoed to the Rose Creek pen with a man who had worked as one of those guards. He had not returned to the site in the sixteen years since his passage through this valley as a protector of wolves. When we reached the pen, tears came to his eyes; he confessed that this had been one of the most meaningful jobs of his life.

His guard duties should have ended on March 22, 1995, when the pen was opened to release the wolves. But two days passed before 10M and the pup walked out. Four days after that, the alpha female ran out, perhaps spurred on by 10M's howling. The trio started their passage into this valley and beyond, helping their species reclaim Yellowstone and the northern Rocky Mountains.

After years of neglect, the pen is now an overgrown one-acre plot surrounded by a ten-foot high, chain-link fence bent and twisted by a couple of fallen trees. I have accompanied numerous groups to the pen. When people entered the historic and deteriorating enclosure, many fell silent as though stepping into a place of worship. Some cried, like that guard. Such strong reactions impressed on me the importance of wolves and how powerful our need is for these symbols of wild freedom. Those moments fueled my desire to advocate for wolves.

Leo and I leave our view of Druid Peak and join Mary and Karen. The four of us pass a series of wallows, dusty circles bison have rubbed bare of grass. The wallows are linked by an animal trail, like dark gems on a necklace.

Just beyond nature's jewels we hear the purr of sandhill cranes from somewhere in the valley below. Captivated by that almost-prehistoric sound, I stop and sit, hoping to spot those big birds. As I study the valley, my partners continue on.

The floor of the Lamar Valley curves up to Specimen Ridge on one side and Druid Peak on the other, forming a wide U, the signature of the passage of ancient glaciers. Back then, everything that makes this view so captivating— the sage-covered valley floor, the winding Lamar River, massive Druid Peak, and Specimen Ridge with its petrified treasures—lay buried beneath thousands of feet of ice.

Those glaciers formed near present-day Cooke City just east of here. They grew slowly, as more snow fell in winter than melted in summer. As they formed, the glaciers flowed down the valleys of the Lamar and Yellowstone Rivers. They passed through what would become Gardiner, leaving glacial erratics sitting today on the school's athletic field and around many homes. The glaciers finally ended their travel in Paradise Valley, about thirty-five miles north of Gardiner.

The glaciers receded after the climate warmed, about 15,000 years ago. They left behind a Lamar Valley floor covered with soil that retains water only to a shallow depth. Water-hungry trees don't like that soil. But grasses do. And those grasses draw the big grazers that make this valley famous—and full of predators.

This wildlife-filled valley also drew humans, who followed the wide corridors carved by glaciers. Native American hunters made the first passages, arriving on foot 11,000 or so years ago. By 1840 members of the Shoshone and Bannock Tribes who lived on the Snake River plain in today's Idaho came as a matter of necessity. The local bison they depended upon for food, clothing, tools, and shelter had been hunted to extinction by Native Americans and whites, according to historian Aubrey Haines.

Hungry and desperate, the Native Americans followed what is now called the Bannock Trail into Yellowstone. They forded the Yellowstone River near Tower Fall and went through the Lamar Valley, continuing east to the Great Plains of Montana where bison still roamed. But by the late 1800s, white hunters had exterminated those bison too, decimating forever the treasure at trail's end—and a way of life.

After the Native Americans came Euro-Americans. One of the first whites to pass through this valley was John Colter, a former member of the Lewis and Clark expedition. In 1807, at the age of thirty-five, he had enough skill and daring to solo a 500-mile circuit through Yellowstone in winter. He carried a thirty-pound pack and covered up to twenty miles a day. Colter followed part of the Bannock Trail through this valley in search of Native Americans willing to trade furs he could sell elsewhere.

Colter was the advance guard of trappers that swarmed into the Yellowstone region from 1822 to 1840, seeking beaver pelts that could be made into coveted hats. They found few beavers here, but trapped the animal almost to extinction in other parts of the West.

One of the trappers was Osbourne Russell, who first visited the Lamar Valley in 1835. Like so many later visitors—including the four of us heading for the knob—he fell in love with this wonderland. Russell returned four times to what he called "Secluded Valley." A different sort of trapper, he was literate and wrote about his passages. His journals provides valuable firsthand insights about other people who have passed through here.

Russell presents, for example, a unique view of the Sheep Eater Indians who lived in the Lamar Valley. Though other writers described these people as stunted and miserable and barely eking out an existence in this harsh land, Russell found the band that he met—about two dozen men, women, and children—to be healthy and thriving.

Yellowstone's Sheep Eaters, according to the *Atlas of Yellowstone,* had working dogs, "large, robust, wolf-like animals" that would mate with wolves. The dogs carried and pulled loads and drove into traps the bighorn sheep the Sheep Eaters used for food, clothing, and bow making. The Indians so loved their dogs that they fed them before taking food themselves. "A dog was often sacrificed when its owner died—so the two could be buried together."

About thirty years after Russell and the other trappers departed, prospectors began their passage through Yellowstone. One party of five, for example, arrived in the summer of 1870, explored the Lamar Valley, and made the gold strike that brought the Cooke City mines.

Just two years later, this valley became part of the world's first national park, a great concept that no one knew how to implement. Neither philanthropists nor the government offered money to protect the park's wildlife. Poachers proliferated. Much of the killing took place on the wide-open floor of the Lamar Valley, below the place where I now sit. Miners on their way to those Cooke City mines took wildlife. So did squatters who lived illegally in the park, hoping the government would come to its senses and release some of this land to settlers.

By 1875 park superintendent Philetus Norris was appalled, writes Haines, by the slaughter of elk, deer, antelope, and bighorn sheep. Five years later the park took a first step to stop poaching: Harry Yount was hired as gamekeeper and lived alone for the winter in a cabin on the eastern edge of this valley, at the confluence of Soda Butte Creek and the Lamar River. This was tough duty; Yount lasted only one year. In his resignation, he wrote that a lone man could not possibly protect all the wildlife in the Lamar Valley.

But no additional protection was forthcoming, and park bison fell to poachers. By 1901 less than two dozen bison remained in all of Yellowstone. To reinvigorate that decimated population, genetically pure bison were brought to the Lamar Valley and a captive herd was raised on what came to be called the Lamar Buffalo Ranch. This valley was fenced from near the bunkhouse all the way to the Lamar River. Within that enclosure, timothy grass—a non-native plant—was grown for hay. The ranch hands who tended the bison ate and slept in the bunkhouse.

No one sleeps in the bunkhouse now that the ranch is a teaching center for Yellowstone Forever—unless seminar participants are exhausted from a long day in the field, satiated with dinner, and lulled by a presenter. But that historic building is still the heart of the ranch. When Mary and I made our passage through this valley, living at the ranch, only six of us stayed all season—four volunteers, the ranch manager, and the district park ranger. When the ranch was free of seminar participants, our tiny group often congregated in the bunkhouse to enjoy communal dinners, play board games, or view photographs of someone's recent adventure. Simple living and companionship made fast friends of perfect strangers.

Researchers were the next group to pass through the Lamar Valley. One of the first was Adolf Murie. In 1937, he and his assistants collected and analyzed more than 5,000 pieces of coyote scat. He learned that coyotes ate grass, pine nuts, rose seeds, strawberries, mushrooms, blueberries, and Oregon grape. They also consumed four kinds of bugs; twenty types of birds, fish, and snakes; twenty-four different small mammals; as well as twelve kinds of large mammals. When I discovered that list during the time Mary and I cooked our own meals at the ranch, I laughed out loud: Murie's coyotes ate better than we did.

As Leo, Karen, Mary, and I continue our climb toward Karen's knob, we wander through knee-high wildflowers in a blast of bloom. We find a stand of willow, the plants at or near the edges browsed down by elk. The plants in the center—a more dangerous place to dine now that wolves are back—are noticeably taller. I can't help but see this as more evidence for the trophic cascade theory. Continuing on, we reach 8,000 feet of elevation and enter the rugged territory of whitebark pine.

When we finally reach our destination, thick gray clouds have filled the sky, and the temperature has fallen. The wind shakes and chills us with each gust. We take shelter behind thick pines and dig into our packs for extra clothes and food. We snuggle into jackets, pull up hoods, and settle down to devour a lunch of crackers, cheese, and fruit; a meal Murie's coyotes would probably ignore.

As we eat we share stories from our adventures at the ranch. How about that winter when the snowfall was so heavy that we shoveled snow all day, only to have a thirty-mile-per-hour wind lay down three-foot drifts by morning? The groans beneath the pines sound as loud as they did back then. Do you remember when we were in the parking lot and the Lamar Canyon pack walked past one side of the ranch while on the other side the Mollie's pack walked in the opposite direction? The memory of being sandwiched between wolves thrills us again. What about the time that bison calf was hit and killed by a visitor's pick-up, and we helped the district ranger sled it into the valley so predators could eat in peace? The solemn spirituality of the touching farewell we gave that bison returns.

Warmed by friendship and nourished by food, we pack up and say goodbye to the knob. Heading down a steep slope, I see the Buffalo Ranch, tiny in the distance, yet so large in our lives. As Mary and my co-workers-turned-friends continue, I reach for a nearby sagebrush. Between my thumb and forefinger, I rub its tiny gray-green leaves, squeeze them like worry beads, and they give up their slick, scented oil. I bring the leaves to my nose and inhale, holding my breath, trying to keep the aroma of this secluded valley within me. Then I exhale until my lungs are empty. I repeat this several times, and each time I feel more connected to the Lamar Valley. To all the people who have passed through here before me, searching for sustenance, riches, knowledge, or experience.

As I start my walk again, I think of Osbourne Russell, that literary trapper so smitten by this valley. He wrote, "For my own part I almost wished I could spend the remainder of my days in a place like this where happiness and contentment seemed to reign in wild romantic splendor."

When I first read those words, I realized that a similar feeling drove Mary and me, after three winters in this valley and thirty-five years in Oregon, to leave our family, friends, home, and security. Gardiner was as close as we could get to Yellowstone and this valley where we too hope happiness and contentment will always reign.

19

The Beetle and the Pine

———

In pre-dawn gray, the glow from our car headlights washes over the yellow walls of Golden Gate Canyon. While I drive, Leo, Mary, and I debate abandoning today's planned hike to the summit of Sepulcher Mountain. Leo predicts the haze from fires in Washington and Oregon will obscure the view from the 9,646-foot summit. But, Mary retorts, summer is flying by—half of August is gone—and we may not get another shot. You never know, I add, when the first snow will blanket Yellowstone.

I don't reveal my private agenda: I want to stand atop each mountain visible from our dining room window. We climbed 10,969-foot Electric Peak eleven years ago, when Mary and I returned to Yellowstone intent on making new memories. We have bushwhacked all over the flat top of Mt. Everts. In a week, we will hike to the summit of Bunsen Peak. That leaves just Sepulcher Mountain.

We decide to go for the summit. I park the car at the trailhead and we step out, don jackets against the morning chill, and start walking north as the sun sneaks over Terrace

157

Mountain. Before we've gone a quarter mile, we hear a wavering howl behind us.

"That's a wolf!" Leo says.

We stop dead in our tracks and turn around. We and the wolf are silent. Then a second howl, this one longer. With no discussion, the three of us, hoping for a glimpse, dash in the direction of the howl. Atop a small hill we stop to listen, but our panting is the only sound we hear.

Then comes yipping. "That's coyotes," Mary says, as more yips join in.

"Do you think the first one was a wolf?" Leo asks.

"Could the first have been a wolf," I wonder aloud, "and then the coyotes replied?"

Were it some other morning we would wait and watch and answer these questions. That's how hikes become meanders. But this is not our usual meander; it's a twelve-mile round-trip climb, with a car shuttle at both ends.

Leaving our questions unanswered, we turn away and proceed along the narrow trail toward Sepulcher. We soon ascend to a large, golden meadow we will follow almost to the mountaintop. In the distance, on another ridge descending from Sepulcher's summit, we spot a herd of elk. Through binoculars, Mary sees that they have spotted us too. The elk gather and begin moving past a large aspen grove. One by one they disappear down the opposite side of the ridge.

I'm captivated by the sight of massive Electric Peak in the distance. Above the forest blanketing its flank, the snow-free peak displays swathes of black, gray, tan, and white cut by a horizontal belt of red.

Leo whispers emphatically, "Look over there." He points toward the ridge the elk just left. "That's a grizzly!"

We watch the grizzly climb the ridge. At the top, the bear lumbers along, and then, sadly for me, disappears down the other side. That moment of sadness is replaced by one of gratitude for living near a place where we can hike, hear wolves and coyotes, see elk and grizzly, and be awestruck by a mountain.

"That's the perfect way to see a grizzly," Leo says, "distant and safe." I nod my head in agreement, remembering the two distant grizzlies we saw courting in May when we stood on nearby Terrace Mountain.

As we continue up Sepulcher, the switchbacks crossing the meadow grow shorter and steeper. When we break to catch our breath, Leo points to a stand of trees just ahead, and says, "Look at those whitebark pine." Some of the pines are dead with gray skeletal branches silhouetted against sun and haze, others are healthy, green, and bushy.

As Mary and I look where he's pointing, he adds, "Listen to all the Clark's nutcrackers in there. It's almost like something out of Hitchcock's movie 'The Birds.' They love whitebark pine nuts."

As we near the top of Sepulcher, the trail enters a dark whitebark pine forest, an eerie backdrop where life and death dance. Leo says this is a perfect location for a grizzly daybed. He stops beside a lush whitebark, squats below the lowest limbs, and declares, "Oh, look at this. Here's one. See how it's been cleared out in there? And the multiple exits. I'll bet this is a daybed."

While I'm excited by this find, I can't help but wonder at the wisdom of poking around in a grizzly's bedroom. This isn't what I would call *distant and safe*. I finger the top of the bear spray canister hanging from my pack's waist belt.

Once Mary and I convince Leo to leave the daybed, the three of us ascend the last stretch to the peak, a jumble of gray volcanic boulders freckled with orange and yellow lichen, amid patches of ground-hugging greenery. As expected, haze from distant forest fires obscures the view. Instead of gawking at a panorama of mountains, forests, grasslands, and the Yellowstone River, we clamber among the rocks.

We're not alone; a golden-mantled ground squirrel scampers toward a boulder. Its eyes are on us, and its mouth is filled with a whitebark pine cone that's bigger than its head. The squirrel traces a crack to the top of the boulder and with a disdainful flick of its tail disappears down the other side.

The squirrel reminds me to look at the ground. When I do, I see pine cones stripped of their seeds laying on a rock. This squirrel's dining rock is surrounded by scattered purple and brown cone debris and clumps of the whitebark needles in their distinctive clusters of five.

Whitebark pines grow slowly and live long. The oldest documented whitebark anywhere lived for a thousand years. Whitebark in Yellowstone need seventy-five to one hundred years just to start bearing cones like the ones on that rock. And all around us on Sepulcher, all around Yellowstone, all around the West these trees are falling to the mountain pine beetle.

The beetle, about the size of a grain of rice, is a native insect that has hitchhiked north as whitebark pines have colonized the northern Rocky Mountains, write Jesse Logan and William MacFarlane in a journal article. The problem with the insect—from the tree's perspective—is that the beetles reproduce by drilling a hole in the tree all the way to the phloem, the layer that carries life-sustaining nutrients. Once there, they lay eggs. After the eggs hatch, the larvae eat their way out of the tree, producing even more holes. The invaders and their offspring create so many holes that the tree can't get adequate nutrients through the riddled phloem and dies.

But the drilling and egg laying are just the first clash of the battle. The pines fight back, try to repel the beetle invasion by producing more resin. The beetles counterattack by introducing a fungus that not only overwhelms the trees' defenses but also feeds the beetles' offspring. This one-two punch reinforces the beetles and knocks out the pines.

Though this battle between pine and beetle is natural, Logan and MacFarlane say that humans have handed the beetle the advantage. As human-caused climate change raises temperatures all year long, beetles live longer and produce more offspring. The result: an outbreak of mountain pine beetles that has spread farther and killed more trees than scientists ever thought possible.

The death of those trees matter, say the authors, because the whitebark pine is a keystone species, critical to this ecosystem and its occupants.

Let's start with that unseen chorus of Clark's nutcrackers we heard on our way to the summit. Whitebark pine seeds are one of that bird's most important foods. To get the goodies, a nutcracker must tear apart a whitebark's tough cones. After reaching the seeds, the bird flies away, carrying batches. It buries the seeds in scattered caches where it hopes to feed later in the year. A single Clark's nutcracker can cache up to 98,000 seeds in a single season, according to one researcher. But the birds don't find all that buried treasure. Seeds not eaten can sprout and expand the forest. The Clark's nutcracker is the Johnny Appleseed of whitebark pine.

Nutcrackers aren't the only animals hungry for the pine's seeds. Squirrels, like that one we saw on the summit, also rip into the cones and stockpile seeds. The mounds they make beneath the pines attract grizzlies. The grizzly we saw go over the ridge may have been searching for stashes to raid.

Pregnant grizzlies need the pine's fatty seeds before they enter their dens for the winter. The amount of pine seeds an expectant mother eats can determine the health of her developing cubs. If she eats too few seeds, her cubs may not survive. Dead cubs mean fewer grizzlies. The loss of whitebark pines is just one of the reasons scientists say that Yellowstone's grizzlies should not be delisted from the protection of the federal Endangered Species Act.

Elk also benefit from whitebark. When they calve among pines in late spring or early summer, the forests protect them from harsh weather and hide them from hungry predators that would love a meal of tender young elk.

Finally, say Logan and MacFarlane, we humans benefit. Most of the water in the West's rivers comes from winter and spring snows. Whitebark pine forests high on the mountainsides shelter snow from the wind and shade it from the sun. The protection means snow takes longer to melt and provides a more prolonged, consistent flow of precious water.

Thus, as the whitebark pine goes so goes the Greater Yellowstone Ecosystem (GYE). This leads to a troubling question: How likely is it that whitebark pine forests will lose the battle with the beetle and stop providing these life-giving ecological benefits?

The answer is uncertain, say the authors. "A disturbance of this magnitude in whitebark pine is unprecedented in the ecological history of the GYE." They speculate that the pine may not be able to adapt its way out of danger. But they respect this resilient survivor: "Whitebark pine is a tough species that has evolved to withstand some of the harshest environmental conditions on the planet."

The battle between whitebark pine and beetle shows no signs of abating. Only time will reveal the outcome. Meanwhile we must learn to live with barren expanses of dead whitebark. And we must accept our part in their demise and work to correct human-caused climate change.

I'm pleased that we reached the summit of Sepulcher Mountain, the last on my dining-room-window list. I'm even glad that the haze from the fires diminished the view. Had this been a typical Yellowstone bluebird day, we would have been dazzled by a 360-degree panorama. We could have missed the squirrel and the whitebark pine seeds that led me to ponder the beetle and the pine.

Their battle amazes me, saddens me, and reminds me that no matter how wild and rugged Yellowstone appears, this wonderland teeming with wolves and coyotes, elk and grizzly, squirrels and nutcrackers—and mountain pine beetles—is a delicate ecosystem that humans, whether living nearby or far away, can alter in destructive and permanent ways.

20

One Last Breath

––––

As August burns on, Mary and I are amazed at how the number of tourists keeps swelling. Park attendance is rushing to set another in a series of annual records. Yellowstone roads are jammed; driving is hazardous. Most roadside attractions along the Grand Loop, the park's main road, are crowded; parking can be impossible.

But we have a secret weapon in our search for seclusion: backpacking. Yellowstone National Park covers more than two million acres but has only about 300 designated backcountry campsites. Each one offers plenty of open space with not another soul in sight.

On this current three-day backcountry trip, we have come to a complete halt at the bottom of the Grand Canyon of the Yellowstone. While noisy sightseers at Artist's Point and Uncle Tom's Trail jostle for a glimpse of the Yellowstone River and its falls, we have this quiet place to ourselves. Our campsite sits on a flat bench the size of a football field about forty feet above the river. Convenient conifers shade our tent. From here we can stroll down a gentle trail to the Yellowstone

River where an intimate white gravel beach awaits, both ends guarded by active—and impassible—thermal features.

We are on that beach and will stay here all day. I will journal, and every hour or so I'll photograph, hoping to capture colorful changes created by Yellowstone's mesmerizing blend of sun and clouds. Mary has nestled into her place of power on the beach where previous hikers built low backrests with river rock. She is soaking in the river the ankle she twisted a week ago on another hike. We hope that a couple of days of river therapy will make the five-mile hike up and out of here less painful than the trek in.

While she soaks, I take in this ancient thermal basin sliced by a river. I am spellbound by the morning sun sparkling on water and by the towering canyon walls, variegated with brilliant green, yellow, and orange.

A spot midway between Mary and the runoff from a bubbling thermal feature calls me. I drift over, throw off my clothes, and wade into the river. I splash my face, arms, and chest in the shocking-cold water. Though our rule of thumb is to never turn down a dip in a pristine river while backpacking, I'm not yet ready to plunge into this one, a favorite we've come to know and love over the years.

The Yellowstone River, 692 miles long and every inch undammed, begins on the Continental Divide south of the park and snakes through the Thorofare in the park's southeastern corner. It feeds Yellowstone Lake and is the lake's only outlet. It broadens through wildlife-rich Hayden Valley, gathers speed, drops over the picturesque Upper and Lower Falls, and rushes into this Grand Canyon that it has cut over millennia. Within that twenty-four-mile-long canyon we sit, insignificant next to the 1,200-foot-high multi-colored walls.

Delighted to be here, I step from the river and settle onto the gravel to observe, photograph, and journal.

10:30 a.m., 84 degrees

A bee lands on the page. We stare at each other as he makes his way along a sentence—past the subject, over the verb, and onto an adverb. If he's an editor, then he's the enemy of honest journalling. I bend forward and gently blow the bee off the page. He buzzes away in Mary's direction.

From my right comes the constant rumble of a thermal feature: sulfur-scented steam billows from two dinner-plate-sized holes in the river bank. Below those openings, steaming water flows to the Yellowstone. I stand, walk to where the river receives the runoff, and step in. "Hey," I yell to Mary, "there's warm water here if you want it for your ankle."

She points to her own sweet mix, laughs, and shouts back, "Hot water! I can't believe it. This place has everything a girl could want." I grin as she dowses herself in the therapeutic mixture.

1:45 p.m., 88 degrees

The sun hangs high in a cloudless southern sky. Strong, vertical sunlight washes out some of the bright green, orange, and yellow in the canyon walls. Shadows from small clusters of trees along the river bank add new color to the changing tapestry.

A dry, warm wind rustles downstream, rippling the river's surface and scattering the sun's diamonds. A grasshopper flies by leaving CLACKETY, CLACKETY, CLACKETY dangling in its wake. Having sat unencumbered for a few hours, I reach out to feel the clothes I scoured in the river an hour ago. Bone dry. I pull on the protection of long pants, long sleeved shirt, and a hat.

2:30 p.m., 90 degrees

The summer sun, unfiltered by clouds, bears down. When I face upriver, the wind threatens to steal my hat. As I tug on the brim, a bright red dragonfly buzzes by, dipping and rising, inspecting the beach home we share. As it flits away, I listen to the canyon's chorus: the rustling of wind in the trees and lapping of water on the bank. I feel the magic of solitude and stillness.

3:45 p.m., 90 degrees

Mary and I awaken from a nap, having sprawled on the coarse, white gravel, fully dressed, shoulders touching, drugged by the touch of the heat and the whisper of the river. Shadows have lengthened on the cliff across the river. I sit up and study three seedlings, each perhaps two feet tall and growing straight and true from a forty-five-degree slope. I marvel at their will to live.

Shading my eyes, I stare skyward and discover clouds, some in the shape of a giant horsetail. Others are thicker and taller, sails on a pirate ship, moving east, high above the canyon. A cricket chirps unseen from the cool shade of a nearby boulder. A duck, wings whooshing, zips upstream, barely a foot above the river. What's the rush?

Lounging here all day embodies the travel philosophy Mary and I have grown into over the years: the slower you go, the more you see. When driving a car, a mile can zip by in about a minute. If riding a bicycle, a mile rolls by in four or five. But as we hike in the backcountry, a mile takes thirty minutes and even that can feel too fast.

5:05 p.m., 88 degrees

The clouds have unionized. No longer separate little puffs, they have banded together, flexing billowing muscles, forming thick masses with battleship-gray bottoms and few breaks of blue. They cover more than half the sky and drift slowly eastward, resisting the wind, demanding more time to block the sun.

The clouds diffuse the light and the river turns a darker green, creeps toward ominous. But the green, yellow, and orange of the opposite bank grow richer, revealing layers, striations hidden until the light of now. What is the story behind the flows that dumped these colorful deposits again and again?

6:00 p.m., 84 degrees

There is so much to learn. So much to see, hear, taste, smell, feel. What I don't know about this place—this short segment of a grand canyon—fills volumes. The little I do know fills my senses and my heart.

After a day of sitting with the Yellowstone River, I decide that if I had the good fortune to choose the place where I could die, this is it: lying beside cool green water on coarse white gravel, listening to the wind and the rumble of thermal features, inhaling the pungent smell of sulfur one last time, and then letting go, exhaling, my long last breath moving downstream with the wind and water.

21

Eyes Wide Open

———

It's early morning, and several days since we took refuge in the Grand Canyon of the Yellowstone. Mary and I are now back among the crowds, part of a group huddled on the gray, plastic-lumber boardwalk near one of the many colorful thermal features in the much-visited Upper Geyser Basin. As other sightseers parade by, I can look across the basin and the Firehole River to the Old Faithful Inn and the windows of Robert Reamer's office, where I spent a few days writing last month.

Today, Mary and I are working, co-supporting a Yellowstone Forever field seminar, driving nine participants wherever the instructor, Lisa Morgan, directs. We will also accompany the group on hikes—and energetic Morgan likes to hike. These are the same duties we had during the winters at the Lamar Buffalo Ranch. But now that we live in Gardiner and don't stay at the ranch, we have no cabins to clean. And, since it's summer, we have no snow to shovel. Hallelujah!

Mary and I and the participants listen intently to Morgan, a geologist who recently retired from the U.S. Geological

Survey. She is shorter than everyone in our group, her body thin and wiry. But after a long career of hefting rocks, she's probably stronger than most of us. On her back rides a stuffed green pack. She wears sky-blue pedal pushers and a matching hat with a wide brim turned down on the sides and pushed up in the front and back.

Morgan explains that the thermal features in Yellowstone developed because of a hot spot within the Earth and the movement of the North American Plate—one of the immense jigsaw puzzle pieces that make up our planet's crust.

"Imagine," she says, "that the hotspot is a huge gas burner." As the North American Plate moves over the hotspot, the intense heat reaches the rocks and water passing ever so slowly above. Rocks melt, forming and filling immense chambers with magma. Subterranean water heats up, and like steam pouring out of a boiling teakettle, must go somewhere. It rises to the surface, carrying minerals and microbes and creating the colorful and captivating thermal features that fill this and other basins in the park.

Morgan calls her approach to geology "science with eyes wide open." And she does keep our eyes—and our minds—wide open as she leads this seminar that she created to focus on tracking that hotspot.

Morgan tells us that the North American Plate moves over the hotspot a little more than an inch a year. When she says that is about the same rate your toenails would grow in a year if you let them, our group breaks into raucous laughter that draws stares from nearby camera-clicking visitors. Morgan adds that while that may seem infinitesimally small, over a million years those inches add up to about twenty-six miles of movement. The plate's plodding passage resulted in this mysterious landscape worth protecting as a national park.

Because of the incredible heat of that hotspot, Yellowstone has risen—the Upper Geyser Basin sits at over 7,300 feet of elevation. But the North American Plate is still moving, and as Yellowstone inches beyond the heat, this region will cool and sink. The much-loved thermal features all around us—deprived of their heat source—will cool. They will dry and lose their colors. Eventually Yellowstone will resemble the landscape south of Idaho's Island Park: flat, lower in elevation, covered with sagebrush, and nary an active thermal feature in sight.

Mary asks Morgan, "Should we call our families and tell them to get out here right away, before the thermal features disappear?"

Morgan laughs and says, "No they've got plenty of time. This change could take as much as several million years."

"That's a relief," Mary says, dramatically drawing the back of her hand across her forehead. The group chuckles their agreement.

On the next day, our mobile seminar hikes along a gravel service road that climbs Mt. Washburn. Our goal is to hike to the 10,243-foot summit and down the other side before dark, keeping our eyes wide open and learning about geology as we go. I walk at the rear of the group, to make sure we don't leave anyone behind. Mary is in the middle, Morgan at the front, walking and talking.

Suddenly, Morgan stops and exclaims, "Oh, look at this!" She points down to a basketball-sized rock partially exposed in the road cut, the bank alongside the road. "It's so cool to find these." Her smile fades to a frown of concentration as she studies the exposed earth around the rock. "I can't tell if this was a bomb and came in hot and landed here or maybe it was a hot part of the pyroclastic flow."

I'm not sure what she means, and the blank expression on other faces tells me I'm not alone. Morgan, an attentive teacher, realizes she has lost some of us. Using simpler language, she says that we are walking atop what geologists call a lahar. Morgan identifies this as a lahar because of all the big rocks—like the one she puzzled over—mixed in with layers of smaller material. She explains that volcanic deposits added to water—lots of water—create a lahar. The water can come from the sky, a river, a lake, a melting glacier, or melting snow.

Then she adds a scary image of how lahars overpower humans and their creations. Once volcanic deposits are saturated, a lahar flows landslide fast, up to forty mph. "So, you're not going to outrun them. It takes out buildings, it kills people. They are terrible, terrible events."

After a moment of silence, Morgan exclaims, "I love road cuts because they expose so much. Roads do geologists a favor! Let me tell you about an incredible pumice quarry just south of Island Park." Digging in that quarry exposed perfect cross sections of eons of volcanic flows from Yellowstone. The cross sections have beautiful ash deposits between them. "It was an outstanding outcrop." Morgan stops and smiles, a geologist recalling the sight of nature's handiwork and history. "So, what did they do? They finished quarrying and then sprayed concrete all over those beautiful exposures." She shakes her head. "And then they put rocks on them and made the quarry into a housing development."

She explains that quarries and road cuts that expose geologic history have stirred debate among geologists. Some believe that such irreplaceable geologic examples should be saved. Designating Yellowstone as a park, for example, preserved its amazing features. A way to do this outside the park, she says, would be to create something like a National Geologic Historic Register on which rare and exceptional geologic formations could be placed and protected, similar to Reamer's Old Faithful Inn's listing on the National Register of Historic Places.

Morgan turns her attention to another large rock and spends time outlining ways this boulder could have formed and come to rest here. She admits to not knowing which, if any, of her scenarios are correct. Then she says, "I love rocks because they can always stump me, and I have to figure them out."

We finally start to move. I'm relieved because at the pace we're going I wonder if we'll ever get over this mountain today. Onward and upward we go—for about twenty yards—until Morgan stops beside a boulder about the size of a bass drum. She squats, caresses its smooth surface, ponders in silence, and finally proclaims that this huge rock was ejected in a volcanic eruption and thrown into the air about fifty million years ago.

Mystified, I stare at the rock, and ask her, "How could something that big be thrown like a tennis ball into the air?" Several participants nod their heads in agreement with my question, and I add, "And how long ago is fifty million years anyway?"

Morgan smiles and says, "The forces of the Earth are large. They dwarf humans. And humans think that they can engineer their way out of almost anything." She pauses. "They can't."

To open our eyes even wider to geologic forces, she picks out another rock that nature has somehow sliced in half, exposing the rock's interior and revealing cracks radiating from the center to the edges. She says that in another Yellowstone eruption rocks and blobs were shot almost straight into the air, soared more than a mile high, and fell back to the earth at over 400 miles per hour. By the time they landed they had cooled. That cooling formed distinctive cracks in the rocks, like those in the one she holds in her hand.

Our eyes open wider still when she describes how 640,000 years ago yet another Yellowstone volcano erupted creating a caldera—a mammoth hole—that swallowed a length of mountain range between Mt. Washburn, where we stand, and Mt. Sheridan more than thirty miles away. A mountain range. Swallowed.

Leaving talk of the mountain-eating caldera behind, we walk for quite a distance, until Morgan stops again. She puts her hand above her eyes to shade the sun and points to the peaks of the distant Gallatin Range. John, a participant who is also a working geologist, and Morgan bat around whether there is any Precambrian rock—rock older than 600 million years—in the Gallatin Range. Six-hundred million years?

The Gallatins include Dome Mountain, Antler Peak, Quadrant and Little Quadrant Mountains, and my favorite, Electric Peak, among others. John explains that moving from Dome to Electric, each mountain in the range reveals an increasingly younger geologic time. Dome shows the oldest, Electric the youngest. Each of these mountains formed from a series of shallow oceans that once covered Yellowstone and eventually dried up.

Imagining a mountain arising from the sea, I ask, "When Dome lifted up from the ocean bottom, was north of Dome the shore of an ocean?"

Morgan laughs and exclaims, "Oh, no, no, no!"

Next comes fifteen minutes of eye-widening dialogue between Morgan and John on how the range formed. The Gallatins did not simply arise from an ocean, like bread popping out of a toaster. Instead, several long ocean-followed-by-no-ocean periods occurred. After millions of years, the last of this stack of oceans dried up leaving an immense flat floor made of what geologists call sedimentary rock. As that North American Plate creeped along, tremendous forces that I can't begin to fathom thrust those dried-up ocean bottoms skyward and formed the Gallatin Range. That's why, John adds, you can find fossils of tiny sea creatures on those mountains. Sea creatures on mountains!

We spent four eye-opening days assisting Morgan—one included a hike to the top of Bunsen Peak, another ancient volcano. With that hike and the one up Sepulcher Mountain, I'm happy that I can now say I have stood atop all the mountains we can see from our dining room window.

By the end of Morgan's seminar, I was physically tired and mentally exhausted but exhilarated. I had struggled to understand geologic concepts that challenged my sense of space and time and force. But Morgan's explanations—free of the complicated jargon that she says give geologists job security—made sense. After this field seminar, I will never look at Yellowstone's grandeur in the same way again.

22

Moose-led Walk

———

I open my eyes to the light of a September dawn filtering through tent walls. Slush in my nearby water bottle confirms that the temperature at our camp in the forest beneath Electric Peak dropped below freezing overnight. Trying not to wake Mary, I wiggle out of my warm sleeping bag, slip on sandals, and crawl from the chilly tent. I stand in my long johns and yawn and stretch and watch my breath drift skyward.

I start walking warily toward the bear pole one hundred yards away, where our gear, hung from ropes, swings ten feet above the ground, safe from inquisitive or hungry bears. Secretive shadows stalk thick woods on either side of the trail. "Yo, bear. It's just me," I announce to the shadows. No reply. Thankfully.

I reach the bear pole. Mary's boots and backpack hang from one rope, my boots and pack hang from the other. I lower my gear from its frosty nighttime perch. As I untie my boots and pack from the rope, Mary's voice drifts from the direction of our tent. I guess I did wake her. She is saying something that sounds like, "Hey Rigg, mooo."

I frown, unsure what that means. "What?" I yell back.

"Moo. Obe dere."

I turn toward the distant tent and retort, "I can't understand you." When Mary does not reply, I shrug and begin to lower her pack and boots.

A moment later she grabs me from behind by both elbows. She's breathing hard from moving fast. She turns me to face the Gardner River and says firmly into my ear, "Moose."

Clutching the rope that still suspends her gear, I stare to where she points. Three sets of eyes stare back. A moose family: bull, cow, and calf stand across the river that looks more like a small creek. They are framed by willows and just twenty-five yards away.

"Oh," I say, "Moose. Over there. Now I get you."

The bull lowers his head and swings it from side to side. His massive antlers cut a large swath. His nonverbal message doesn't feel friendly. His size and attitude make me wary, more so than that cow and calf Mary stumbled upon during our meander along the Blacktail Deer Plateau. The presence of a calf for this big bull to protect cranks up my nervousness. My adrenaline fires.

As I continue lowering Mary's pack and boots, I whisper over my shoulder, "If the moose cross that river, we're out of here."

Mary, eyes wide, nods agreement.

As if he heard me, the bull splashes into the river, heading toward the spot where we stand and gawk.

"Here they come," says Mary.

"Grab your stuff!" I yell.

I throw my pack over one shoulder, my tied-together hiking boots over the other, and, still in sandals, hustle toward a trail that bisects a nearby meadow. I glance back to see where Mary is. She's right behind, also in long johns and sandals with gear dangling, blonde hair flying. As we scuttle through frost-covered grasses, my sandaled feet quickly turn wet and cold.

When we reach the trail, we stop and look back, panting. The whole family, with dad leading the way, and mom bringing up the rear, is charging up the same trail where we stand frozen. If I didn't feel so threatened—moose have chased people in the park—I'd laugh at their ungainly gallop.

Frantic, I swivel my head left and right seeking sanctuary. There! On the other side of the meadow a thick stand of conifers! Maybe dad won't be able to get his big rack between those tightly packed trunks.

I point toward the trees and shout, "Let's go!"

Mary and I run clumsily, gear bouncing noisily. We must look as funny to the moose as they do to us.

We reach the trees, slip between the tight trunks, stop, and peer out. We breathe out loud and visible sighs of relief as the moose family trots away from us along the same trail we had sought.

Standing there, cold and relieved, we burst into laughter. Evidently, we had the same escape plans as the moose.

Fall

23

The Ecological Footprint of Wolves

A few weeks after we fled from the moose family, Mary and I jump at the chance to assist Bob Beschta in his field work related to plants, elk, and wolves. His wandering takes him well off trail in areas of Yellowstone where grizzlies travel. Since most grizzly attacks happen to lone hikers, adding the two of us to his group of one, even if we aren't scientists, makes sense.

Since 2001, this Oregon State University professor emeritus has observed firsthand how aspens, cottonwoods, willows, and berry-producing shrubs have begun to recover since wolves returned to Yellowstone. Scientific research has left no doubt in his mind about the beneficial—the ecosystem-saving—presence of wolves. While we are familiar with his research, this is our first opportunity to go into the field with him as he gathers data.

In early morning light we move away from the trailhead and toward the distant hills where we will work on this crisp September day. Beschta points with a hiking pole to some healthy young aspens and willows growing along Glen Creek. If wolves were still absent from Yellowstone, he says, those aspens and willows would be eaten down to the nubs by elk who could dine for as long as they pleased. But fearing wolves, or the threat of wolves, elk have changed where and how they eat. This has allowed plants that were once ravaged by elk to grow six feet tall, a height that research shows is critical. If they can grow that tall, elk browsing no longer threatens the plants' existence. "All aspen and willow need," Beschta says, "is a chance."

Farther along the trail, he stops and points at colorful young aspens growing amidst willows. These aspens interest him because he sees no mature tree, no mother tree, nearby. Though aspens almost always spread as clones from the roots of a mother tree, they can also spread by seeds. Some of the trees he points to are putting on their red, yellow, and orange fall foilage. Others still sport summer green. This variety of colors leads Beschta to believe that the seeds of these aspens came from a variety of sources. "If they were a clone," he says, "they would all look the same."

This stand not only demonstrates that aspens can grow from seed, it also reveals what Beschta calls the ecological footprint of wolves: how the influence of wolves cascades down to the plants of an ecosystem. We have passed three piles of fresh wolf scat along the trail. The scat could be from the 8-Mile wolves since we're in their territory again. Whoever left those calling cards, this evidence of wolves may have kept elk from devastating the willows and young aspens that interest Beschta.

As the aspens and willows have grown along Glen Creek, beavers have settled nearby, since they too love to eat both plants. They have built a dam on the creek, and its pond south of the trail reflects clouds and sky. This pond moistens and softens an increasing area of ground at its edges. Elk do not like feeding on such soft ground, possibly because it slows their escape from wolves. But aspens and willows love moist ground, and without elk browsing fresh sprouts to within an inch of their lives, the stand has grown taller and wider.

Beschta has done much of his research and co-published about twenty-five scientific papers with Bill Ripple. Many of their papers have related to the trophic cascade theory. While they believe that wolves are the main reason some ecosystems have started to recover, other scientists present alternative theories.

A commonly offered alternative is that climate change has helped Yellowstone's aspen, willow, and cottonwood recover. But Beschta doesn't agree. "If you look at our papers, you will see that with almost every one of them we've done a climate assessment of some kind, always considered climate a competing hypothesis." Time after time, Beschta and Ripple arrived at the same conclusion: there is nothing in the climate data that explains the change since wolves were reintroduced. The improvements in the plant communities were too immediate to call climate the cause.

Leaving the trail, we bushwhack across the valley floor, around and through sage, stirring up its invigorating aroma. We rock-hop across Glen Creek to reach a stand of aspens and their recruits—thin saplings growing below a few mature ones.

Beschta sets to work. He removes from his backpack a sliding ruler that will extend to measure trees that are twice as tall as him. He selects recruits and measures their height. At various points along each trunk he determines whether and when the recruit was browsed by elk. He relays this information to Mary, and she records the data in his field notebook.

While Beschta gathers data and Mary records, I do my part by climbing up a sixty-five-degree slope searching for scat (Beschta measured the slope's angle as part of his research). I walk a specific pattern and use two clickers—one to record bison scat and one for elk scat. Then I give Mary the two counts, to provide an indication of how often elk and bison frequent this area.

After Beschta finishes measuring, he scans for conditions that could affect an elk's decision on whether to dine here. Is the visibility poor? Are there conifers or ridges nearby from which wolves could suddenly appear and attack? Are there logs that would impede escape?

Standing among the recruits, he turns a circle, points, and says, "If I'm an elk, I can see one hundred yards that way, one hundred yards this way. I can see approaching wolves. Even if they come out of the woods, I've got a good escape route."

Where he stands, elk may have less reason to fear the presence of wolves and more reason to dine. It's also where the recruits are shortest.

The opposite may be true as well: if a site has factors that make spotting wolves or escape difficult, elk could feel more fear. They could browse less, and aspens, willows, and cottonwoods could grow more. I saw this possible relationship between wolves, elk, and plant growth, this ecology of fear, on our good-bye hike with Karen in the Lamar Valley and in our meander with Leo through the wildlife graveyard along Blacktail Deer Creek.

Beschta wraps up our lesson and his tools and we bushwhack to a stand of six aspens higher up the hillside. Each of these trees is at least one hundred years old, he says. Their trunks are thick and free of branches and leaves until halfway to the top. As he photographs these old-timers for his records, he tells us that some of Yellowstone's aspen stands have been growing in the same places for thousands of years.

He pockets his camera and takes us on a journey through time. First we go back to 1900 when wolves roamed Yellowstone and kept the elk population in check. We would be standing in the cool shade of a full aspen forest, instead of in the sun shining through six, lonely old trees. This grove would be thick with aspens of all sizes, stair-stepping in height from sprouts to mature adults.

But moving forward to say 1940, we would find that thick forest disappearing. Wolves are nowhere—the last one killed over a decade earlier. Hungry elk are everywhere. When adult aspens send up the sprouts intended to one day replace them, elk chomp the tender recruits to within a couple feet of the ground. When next year's growing season rolls around, elk will devour that new growth. Year after year this scenario repeats until the ravaged sprouts no longer have strength to recover. Then the recruits die.

Now, let's travel to the present where we find only aspen of two ages. First are mature trees that sprouted before wolves were killed off—like the one-hundred-year-old survivors we stand among. Second are their recruits that have sprouted since wolves returned in 1995. Seventy years of aspens are missing in this stand. They were consumed by overabundant elk in the absence of wolves.

And if we zip one hundred years ahead, with wolves around to keep elk cautious and their population in check, this grove can become a full forest again with aspens of all sizes, from tiny sprouts to huge adults. It will look as it did in 1900. Thanks to wolves. Beschta suggests that perhaps we should call these trees "wolf aspen" because without the return of wolves, aspen would have disappeared from the landscape in this northern part of the park.

Relaxing during lunch in the shade of aspen, I ask Beschta how he came to believe so strongly in the benefit of wolves in this—or any—ecosystem. He says that after he earned his Ph.D. in watershed management he started teaching and researching at Oregon State. He spent much of his career studying riparian zones—those diverse plant and animal communities that border streams, rivers, and lakes. Over decades he learned, "If you want small mammals, if you want large mammals, if you want birds, if you want pollinators, you better have healthy riparian plant communities."

When he came to visit Yellowstone's Northern Range in 1996, he was shocked to see that the essential riparian areas—especially in the wildlife-filled Lamar Valley—had been transformed and trashed by overgrazing elk.

He returned to Yellowstone five years later to analyze cottonwood growth and disappearance. He found cottonwoods in the Lamar Valley over 200 years old. He saw that those cottonwoods were healthy as far back as when Lewis and Clark crossed our continent. "Furthermore," he says, "coming toward the present, the data indicated that everything was doing fine until the early 1900s when wolves disappear."

The possibility that the eradication of wolves could have led to major ecosystem damage cranked up his curiosity and led to more field work, data analysis, and the partnership with Ripple. Research convinced them that the presence of wolves has been the key to the recovering health of Yellowstone's ecosystem.

The sun is disappearing behind the Gallatin range when we bushwhack to the last stand of the day, a tall, single, old aspen, the limbs on one side leafless. It is surrounded by hundreds of recruits. Some are ten feet tall. Beschta points to the ailing aspen and says that as the recruits grow, they take more water and nutrients from the soil. Deprived of nutrition, the sickly mother will die sooner than if there were no recruits growing below her twisted old branches. I'm touched by how this is similar to the way some human parents sacrifice for their offspring.

As we pack up and start the three-mile return trip to the trailhead, Beschta stops, looks around, smiles, and says, "It's nice to be on a positive ecological story. I've been on so many downers. This one keeps bringing me back."

He's excited by all the young aspen we have walked among today, especially those over the magic six-foot height. He says that we have traipsed through a success story written by wolves. Then he laughs and adds, "Wolves have done more riparian restoration that I ever did in my career."

24

Life and Death Among Wolves

———

The big screen at the front of the darkened room fills with images. A lone male wolf looks up a snowy slope, his gaze intent. On that slope stand seven members of the Lamar Canyon pack, staring back at him, just as intent. Suddenly, the three adults and four pups, tails raised, sprint down the hillside toward the loner.

The presenter of this video is Kira Cassidy. She has worked with the Yellowstone Wolf Project since 2007. Before that she studied wolf territoriality and aggression under Dr. L. David Mech, a world-renowned wolf expert. She points to the lone wolf on the screen and says that he had been trying to approach the Lamars for a few hours. Wolves, she explains, are territorial, and don't like intruders. They post plenty of KEEP OUT signs. One of those signs, their scent marks, can last as long as three weeks. Cassidy has seen wolves dig through deep snow to reach a scent mark. Wolves also howl to claim territory. She speculates that wolves can hear a howl ten to fifteen miles away.

Did this lone wolf miss the scent marks and howls? Did he disregard them? Was he trying to join the pack? Were his hormones driving him to single out one of the pack's females?

Only he knows what compelled him to risk this approach, but when the wolf on the screen sees the seven charging wolves, he knows it's time to skedaddle. He bounds away, sinking into deep snow with each leap. The Lamars, with the advantage of following in his tracks, gain on him. Two black males lead the chase. One, wearing collar number 755M, is the alpha male. The other, 754M, is his bigger brother. Next come four uncollared pups, two males and two females. Bringing up the rear is 06, the pack's alpha female.

Mary and I are viewing this video with about seventy-five others. We are crowded into the meeting room of Dr. Jim Halfpenny's Track Education Center and Museum, a short walk down the hill from our house. Most of the viewers are avid wolf watchers, and many are Gardiner residents. As summer's crowds fade, many of these residents—who have spent the long and busy season earning a living from park visitors—again have time to socialize with neighbors.

Cassidy tells us that this video was shot several years earlier. She has watched this film over and over, often one frame at a time to examine each wolf's behavior. By doing so, she discovered that 06, running behind the pack, is not focused only on the lone wolf. Instead, 06 scans up and down the valley, making sure that her pack will not be surprised if more wolves appear nearby. A murmur of appreciation for the alpha female comes from the audience. Many of us observed firsthand 06's striking intelligence and strong leadership before she was killed.

On the screen, 754M and 755M reach the lone wolf but hesitate to attack, maybe because the intruder is larger than either of them. The pups arrive and glance at the two adults for cues. Almost the size of the brothers, the pups are now traveling with the pack as full-fledged members. But they are inexperienced; Cassidy explains that this may be their first battle.

She has studied how levels of aggression change as wolves mature. For females, the level remains the same over the course of the animal's life. But for males, the level increases with age, making them more and more likely to take part in an aggressive chase like the one on screen.

Suddenly, the brothers attack the lone wolf with no mercy. The pups jump in, the males more ferocious than the females. While keeping an eye out for other wolves, 06 joins the fray. The seven wolves ravage the loner, now on his back in the snow, his body covered by a writhing mass of biting wolves.

In the dim light reflected from the screen, Mary and I look at one another and grimace. We reach for each other's hand. Around us, scattered exclamations reveal that this fierce, seven-against-one assault has unsettled other viewers too.

But the tide turns for the loner when he somehow manages to sit up and bite one of the pups on the head. All four pups back off, leaving the two brothers and 06. Finding room to breathe, the lone wolf stays seated and presents his back to his attackers. Then, for no obvious reason, the three adults stop attacking. The loner stands and starts to move away.

Mary and I sigh in relief, but questions fill my head. How can he move after that onslaught? Is it possible that the Lamars pulled their punches? Was there just not enough fighting power?

In the fatal interactions Cassidy has studied, the killing was usually accomplished by a group of at least four wolves. In this battle, seven wolves attacked. But, she says, the four unskilled pups may not have counted for much. Perhaps the three adults were not sufficient to finish off that big intruder, especially with 06 putting some of her energy toward watching for other wolves.

Or maybe he was just lucky. Cassidy has studied data on 292 aggressive wolf chases that occurred between 1995 and 2011. Seventy-two of those chases turned into attacks. Only thirteen of the attacks resulted in the chased wolf being killed. So this wolf is not the only one to have escaped what could have been a fatal encounter.

For a moment, the Lamars just stand and watch the loner leave. As his walk turns to a trot, the two male pups follow him but make no contact. The youngsters may have been confident enough to escort him out of the area, Cassidy says, because they knew the pack's adults were nearby and ready to help.

Territoriality and aggression like that which has us nailed to the seats of the Track Center's folding chairs has long fascinated humans. Cassidy tells us that Aristotle wrote about bird territoriality. In the 1800s, experiments were conducted with the hypothesis that aggression builds up inside an animal—like a ticking time bomb—until the aggression explodes and the animal attacks. Later, scientists came to believe that aggression is not an internal explosion, it's a reaction to something external. Most recently, scientists have developed a theory that aggression must yield more benefits than costs; there's a payoff for being aggressive.

While the subject of aggression has long been investigated, Cassidy says it wasn't until the 1930s and 1940s that scientists began studying individual wolves and packs in the wild. Biologists would follow a pack for months or even years. But until 1995, few observers had ever witnessed an encounter like the one we are watching.

With the 1995 reintroduction, Yellowstone became the best place in the world to watch wolves. Unlike forested habitat where wolves are difficult to observe, Yellowstone's wide-open grasslands draw elk and the hungry wolves that follow. The white backdrop of winter helps in spotting and filming this life-and-death drama, as renowned videographer Bob Landis did with this encounter.

As the lone wolf distances himself from the Lamar pack, he shows no obvious sign of the attack. No limping, no blood trail. At the scene of the fight the snow is rough and cratered but there is no visible blood. This surprises me but not Cassidy. She has studied many wolves killed by other wolves. From the outside there often appears to be little damage; there's hardly any blood. But, she says, when investigators peel back the fur of the deceased wolf, they find extensive hemorrhaging, damage from canine teeth strong enough to puncture a skull.

This intruder was indeed lucky. Cassidy says that wolves killing other wolves now accounts for up to 70 percent of the known natural causes of wolf death in Yellowstone. That figure has increased over the years. Shortly after reintroduction, when the park's wolf population was small, there were few aggressive encounters. The number of attacks increased as the population grew. Cassidy says that once there is a jump in wolf population, the very next year there is a jump in aggressive interactions.

On the screen, the pack watches the lone wolf cross the frozen Lamar River and leave the territory. As the lights come up and Cassidy reveals that the intruder survived and continued roaming Yellowstone, sighs of relief flow from the audience.

———

Several days went by before my mind stopped replaying troubling scenes from the video. I struggled to accept that such a ferocious and one-sided assault is the natural order. But as a species, wolves have roamed the Earth for millennia. And in all that time as they protected their young, food, and territory from intruders, they have behaved just as they did in the video. Wolves have killed other wolves, but the species has survived. This is just as it should be, regardless of how difficult it is to watch.

But something more difficult to watch and understand is how we humans kill wolves. We eradicated them from

Yellowstone National Park by 1926. By the 1960s, we had wiped out all the wolves in the Lower 48 except those hiding in the woods of northeastern Minnesota.

I have come to believe that humans attack wolves because we compete with them for territory and food. We *Homo sapiens* may try to justify our killing by accusing *Canis lupus* of being evil and greedy, but in the end, we are just cutting the competition. In that sense, our relationship with the wolf is similar to the wolf's relationship with the coyote.

When a Yellowstone wolf pack, the top predator, brings down an elk, each member eats its fill and then moves from the carcass to sleep off the "meat drunk." As the wolves drowse, an opportunistic coyote may sneak in to scavenge. The wolves may pay no mind, chase the coyote, or kill it. If they kill the coyote, they usually don't eat it. The wolves are not hungry; they just ate. They are simply cutting the competition for their hard-won meal. Wolves and coyotes have coexisted—have self-regulated—like this for thousands of years, with careless coyotes losing their lives but their species surviving.

In the case of wolves and humans, we are the top predator. When opportunistic wolves encroach on our livestock—often while we sleep off a meal—we may do nothing, chase the predators away, or kill, but not eat, the wolves.

Human-wolf conflict has proven inevitable because wolves and humans are so similar. Wolves live almost everywhere we do, and both species are territorial. While *Canis lupus* claims territory with scent-marking and howling, *Homo sapiens* use political borders and barbed wire. Wolves and humans like the same meals, and for the same reason: a domestic cow chewing its cud on wide-open public land, for example, is much easier to catch, kill, and devour than a big bull elk, able to defend itself with hooves and antlers. Wolves can bring down that elk because they hunt in packs; they find strength in numbers. So do humans, who cooperate in families and groups. Within every wolf pack or human group there are leaders and followers.

This combination of territoriality, cooperation, and leaders with followers causes wars: wolves fighting wolves—as we saw in the video; humans fighting humans; and, of course, humans warring against wolves. And make no mistake, this is a one-sided war; wolves rarely attack people.

Homo sapiens have spawned a varied and deadly arsenal—including disgusting biological and chemical weapons. We also have bigger—and more devious—brains with which to devise an overwhelming array of negative, false, stereotypes of *Canis lupus*. We create and implement frightening battle plans against wolves. The end result: We can exterminate all the wolves we can find.

Now that's something too gruesome to stand by and watch.

25

Wild Nights

———

I just awoke in our tent from a nightmare. A hammering-heart, sweaty-T-shirt, sleeping-bag-wrapped-around-me-like-an-anaconda nightmare.

In my dream, I had been with some real-life men friends in a decrepit farm house that I had lived in many years ago. We were being burned, hit, shot, and cut by three bullies, guys who had tormented me when I was growing up. Though we outnumbered the bullies, we knew we couldn't beat them. I tried to rally my friends with an impassioned speech that ended with a melodramatic, "Someone may die here tonight."

As Mary sleeps soundly beside me, another endless September night deep in Yellowstone's backcountry creeps along. I give up, sit up, grab my journal, and start writing.

Why is it that my backcountry days are awash with awe and wonder, while the nights can be ruled by dread and fear? Perhaps it's because I'm enclosed in a tent with walls almost as thin as the paper I'm scribbling this on. And out there, on the other side of that flimsy nylon layer, are "bullies": bull bison, bull moose, and bears, all strapping, unpredictable animals that act for their own wild reasons. I'm in their home, out of my element, and afraid of being bitten, gored, stomped, or clawed.

Lying here, blood pounding in my temples, I'm hyper-alert to all night sounds. With every rustle or snap, my body fires a shot of adrenaline, preparing for fight or flight. I wish I had a metal vehicle or a brick house wrapped around me instead of this clammy, blue sleeping bag. While this bag will keep me warm, it will not stop antlers, horns, claws, or teeth.

Though this confession embarrasses me, it's necessary. If I do not own my fears, they own me; they bully me. But when I drag them out of my psyche and force them onto paper, they lose their power. But they don't disappear. These are primal fears. Even in our strong, secure Gardiner home, I occasionally awaken to an unfamiliar scraping or thumping and think: *Is someone or something coming to get me?*

Oh, I know that I'm more likely to accidentally harm myself in my home than I am to be terrorized in this tent by a rampaging grizzly. I'm more likely to be crippled in a car accident than broken by a bison. So why am I awake now, waiting, as it were, for the other paw or hoof to drop? Why even put myself in this situation? Why plan for months and hike for miles only to awaken to heart-thumping fear on some backcountry night?

Perhaps it's because I'm exploring both an external and internal wilderness. There's the real wilderness outside of me that I savor during the day. Then there's my nighttime wilderness of imagination and nightmares, where I'm vulnerable. I cannot fully explore the wilderness outside without exploring the wilderness inside, without removing myself from the walls and windows, doors and locks that keep primal fears contained the rest of the year.

The fears that haunt my nights have been around as long as humans. These fears are our heritage. In caves without doors or locks, our ancestors huddled around fires that they hoped would keep the creatures of the night away. Centuries passed and they learned to build impenetrable buildings that kept animals out. But buildings don't keep primal fears out. So our ancestors kept shooting, trapping, and poisoning any and all creatures that evoked the fight or flight response. Kill the animal; kill the fear.

But tonight, as my heart calms and I hope for sleep to return, I nest in the largest intact ecosystem in the Lower 48. Yellowstone—with the controversial reintroduction of the wolf, once annihilated here by people who hated and feared it—has every predator now that it had before becoming a park. They're all just outside this tent somewhere. And I came here to be near them. To experience the grandeur of their wild home. And to face my fears.

26

Wading Through the Bechler

———

Shouldering forty-pound packs, Mary, Brenda, Fred, and I trudge away from the historic log cabin that houses the Bechler Ranger Station. On a narrow timber, we wobble across a small creek, the first of many water crossings we will encounter over the next four days.

Bechler Meadows, our first-time destination, is a water wonderland in the remote southwestern corner of Yellowstone. With almost eight feet of precipitation every year—the most in the park—much of the Bechler is under water May through mid-July. That—and avoiding Bechler's famed mosquitoes—is why we waited until late-September to traverse the area's sloughs, marshes, ponds, hot springs, creeks, and rivers. Bechler also boasts the highest concentration of waterfalls in Yellowstone—some well over 200-feet high—and we plan to gawk at a few of those too.

Our real entrance into this wet and wild land comes at Bartlett Slough when we leave a shady conifer forest and enter a golden meadow. The footing along the trail grows softer with each step until we reach a wide pool. The passage over the pool is on a log someone placed there. The log is a wooden tightrope about four inches—one boot—wide and twenty-five feet long.

In a flood of testosterone, I volunteer to cross first. Fred asks if I want to use his hiking poles for balance. I shake my head and reach down to grab a couple of long sticks left by others who have crossed. I step onto the log, push a stick into the soft bottom on either side, and start.

This balancing act works until I reach the middle of the log, which is bouncy and wobbly and above the deepest water. Now to touch bottom with the sticks, I have to bend at the waist until my body forms a ridiculous upside-down L. The sticks bend under the pressure, rendering them almost useless: the heavy backpack and bouncing log want to send me into the water. I stop and silently ask myself, *Why didn't I accept Fred's offer?*

As I stand there, my hiking partners shout comments—concerned and comical. Ignoring them, I take a breath, concentrate, and step-by-bouncing-step reach the other side. Dry and relieved, I flop onto the grass.

Mary, Brenda, and Fred cross successfully, each bent into the same pose; it's humorous now that I'm safely across. As we sit on the ground, eat a snack, and stare at the pool, sharing our fear of falling, a batch of young hikers arrive from the direction we are going. They greet us and approach the log in a long, straight line. Without hesitation, the leader, standing tall and without poles, walks quickly across the log. As the rest of the group follows—all upright and pole-free— the four of us look at each other with chagrin.

Mary sums it up: "I'm glad they didn't arrive when I was bent over on that log. I would have been embarrassed and probably fallen in. Sheesh!"

Brenda, Fred, and I nod and laugh in agreement.

Fred has just finished volunteering at the Lamar Buffalo Ranch, his second straight season there. That amounts to about ten months at the ranch, most of that time surrounded by visitors. His ability to do that showcases one of his strengths: determination. He left a successful career as a construction project manager and came to Yellowstone to start anew. He is determined to do whatever it takes to stay here. He has his eye on a job as a seasonal park ranger. His duty will be to manage animal jams caused by roadside appearances of bison, bears, and wolves. His private goal is to help visitors connect with Yellowstone.

Brenda volunteers at the ranch too, on a fill-in basis throughout the year. She lives in Bozeman and pays her bills by working as a nurse. She arranges her schedule so that she has three or four days off in a row. This gives her time to drive the 110 miles one-way to the ranch, volunteer a few days, and let Yellowstone feed her soul.

The four of us leave the crossing and hike along the edge of a forest, with shade on the right, sun-drenched meadow on the left. We reach the next ford, strap on sandals, roll up pants, and wade across. The water is knee-deep, chilly, and refreshing. We joke and laugh. Now that's the way to cross a creek!

As the day lengthens, we approach our first campsite. But to reach it, we must cross Boundary Creek. This crossing log is eight-inches wide and about three feet above the creek. Fred and Brenda traverse with no problem. Mary mounts the log before I do, takes two shaky steps, and slips off into the shallow water. I meet her on the bank when she splashes out of the creek in water-filled boots, grumbling and cursing.

"I'm tired and hungry and right now my balance stinks," she says through a scowl.

"No problem," I say, "I'm feeling the same way. I'd be glad to wade across." Any slip in the backcountry can be dangerous.

Mary looks over at the crossing log, the creek, and Fred and Brenda relaxing on the opposite bank. She shakes her head and mutters, "Oh, okay."

I make a courtly gesture, inviting her to sit on the bank. We remove our shoes, put our sandals on, and wade hand in hand to the other bank through knee-deep water. We keep our sandals on for the short side trail to our campsite on the edge of a meadow with Boundary Creek on one side and willows and forest on the other.

During the night, I wake up and want to take in Yellowstone's nighttime grandeur. I worm free of my sleeping bag and unzip the tent flap that is stiff with September frost. I crawl out, hands and knees rapidly chilling. Still on all fours, I stop and look at the sky. Discomfort fades. The moon is full, the sky clear. A few stars outshine the moon. I stand and slip on sandals. Around me, the meadow's golden grass glows, the frost sparkles. It's so quiet that I can hear the call of Dunanda Falls, tomorrow's destination, a mile and a half away.

Over coffee the next morning, Mary and I stroll the short distance to admire Boundary Creek as it curves silently through the frosted meadow. I have heard that this area supports deer and elk, black bear and grizzlies, moose and muskrats, beavers and otters, bald eagles and osprey, coyotes and wolves. A howl from the Bechler pack would make my trip. Where the pack is today—or any day—is anyone's guess since none of the wolves are now collared, and the Yellowstone Wolf Project rarely travels to this remote region of the park.

Mary and I leave the creek and join Brenda and Fred for the hike to Dunanda Falls. We pass through part of the 8,000-acre Robinson Creek burn that swept through here in 1995. Among the young, dark-green lodgepole pines, pockets of bright yellow aspen gleam. As the trail climbs, willows appear. We round a curve and there's our first animal sighting: a young bull moose chomping willows just off the trail. He swivels his big head, studies us, swallows, and returns to eating. We watch him for a few moments and then slip quietly past.

We reach the bottom of Silver Scarf Falls, a roaring 250-foot cascade that has tossed and piled downed timber on both banks as if those once full-sized trees were twigs. A couple hundred yards later, we arrive at the brink of Dunanda Falls. Dunanda is a Shoshone word for "straight down" and that name fits this site. But it's the rainbow at the base of the 150-foot falls that captures me. When I finally wrench my gaze away, I take in the distant view. No crowds, no buildings, no roads, no noisy motorcycles, just the rumble of the falls, purr of the wind.

What a refreshing change during our first summer living in busy Gardiner and driving our car or a bus along Yellowstone's crowded Grand Loop. I've read that all the development that most people see—the roads, buildings, and parking lots—covers only about 5 percent of Yellowstone. But when I experience sound traveling in the park, I figure that the racket of all the human hubbub ends up invading much more of the wildland. Since the Bechler is one of the rare areas not accessible from the Grand Loop, peace and quiet abound here and soothe us.

By mid-morning, we return from Dunanda Falls, break camp, and head for our next site. The trail cuts through a thick conifer forest and enters an expansive meadow with wide wet areas that we must avoid or have our boots sucked into the muck. This meadow, covered with grass and sliced by a creek, reminds me of Hayden Valley—without the bisecting road.

After crossing the meadow, we come upon the Bechler River. Its smooth surface reflects the conifers that line the opposite bank. At the designated ford, the quiet river is at least forty-feet wide. We can't determine how deep it is. Since Mary has been hiking in sandals, she simply rolls up her pants legs and wades in.

Walking away, our canary in the mine looks over her shoulder and assures us, "The water is cold and clear. I can see where I'm going." A moment later she yells back, "I'm following the buildup of gravel on the bottom."

When she reaches the middle of the river, the extra height from the gravel keeps her backpack just above the water. But as she continues across, the gap between her pack bottom and the water slowly but surely increases. One by one, Brenda, Fred, and I wade in and follow Mary's submerged trail. My feet are burning from cold by the time I step onto the grassy bank.

We make camp in the forest and enjoy a warmer night's sleep. Awakening to a second Bechler morning, I amble to the river and plop down on grass moist with dew. I listen to the trickle of the solitary riffle in this stretch of the river. I stare at the clouds and sky and conifers reflected in slow-moving water. The reflection looks like an oil painting; the ripples mimic the strokes of an artist's brush.

My hiking partners arouse me from this art appreciation, and we start marching to Colonade Falls, our last stop on this trip. We quickly enter the Bechler River Canyon. In some places, the trail along its floor is a one-person-wide path weaving through jumbles of volcanic rocks. At others, the trail widens, the sinuous Bechler River on one side and gray cliffs softened by splashes of yellow lichen on the other.

Climbing gradually, we pass many old Douglas firs that remind me of forests Mary and I hiked while living in Oregon. These trees—some of the largest in the park—became giants because of that eight feet of precipitation that falls here. They remained giants because they escaped the devastating fires of 1988. As we continue through the firs with streams flowing past them and ferns growing under them, I feel a twinge of homesickness, the first I've felt since moving here.

As a long-time Oregonian, I guess I should not be surprised that trees, water, and ferns have brought it on.

Soon we hear the roar of upper and lower Colonade Falls. Both flow wildly, even though it's September. Falls like these and Dunanda abound in the Bechler, caused in part by the region's unique lava flow. Here, debris from ancient volcanic eruptions did not soar into the air and crash to earth, as Lisa Morgan described it doing elsewhere in Yellowstone. Instead, according to another geologist, David Rodgers at Idaho State University, lava—as hot as 1500 degrees Fahrenheit—oozed across the ground and formed two hard volcanic plateaus from which waterfalls and cascades crash and carve into softer meadows below.

During lunch, we are treated to occasional sprays of mist from Colonade Falls. I regret that this is as far as we will go in the Bechler Canyon this time. Tomorrow we return to the trailhead. We will follow a different trail, one easier to navigate than the route in. Though it won't be any drier. But we have become old hands at wading through the Bechler. And a wide and sturdy suspension bridge over the final creek will surely help.

———

A few days after our return, as I read about the history of the Bechler, I realize how lucky we are to have this wet and wild part of Yellowstone. All that water we traipsed through once attracted people who coveted this area for something other than a "useless" park.

Fifty years after Yellowstone became a park, Addison Smith, a representative from Idaho, introduced a bill into the U.S. House of Representatives to turn the Bechler region into an irrigation reservoir for Idaho farmers. But, according to historian Aubrey Haines, after William C. Gregg explored the Bechler and "found more falls and cascades than in all known parts of the park," Smith's bill died a much-deserved death.

But Smith didn't give up. A few years later he tried to have the park boundaries changed so that the Bechler would no longer be considered within Yellowstone. Then the precious water would be Idaho's for the taking. Thankfully, that attempt failed, too.

Here's how Haines closes his chapter on the attempt to plunder Yellowstone's water: "For the moment, the park is safe. Given the right set of economic circumstances, however, the old need for irrigation water (so like the drunkard's thirst) could again generate schemes inimical to the purposes for which the area was set aside."

The need for water Haines hints at will surely become a problem. In 2003 and again in 2013, the Government Accountability Office (GAO) completed a study on problems our country faces with freshwater. The agency estimated the extent of future water shortages in all fifty states. In 2003, the GAO estimated that Montana, Idaho, and Wyoming would have water shortages in parts of their states over the next decade. By 2013 Montana's estimate had worsened to predict statewide shortages over the coming decade. During a recent summer, Montana and Idaho were two of the states with the worst drought conditions in the nation. Yet water demand in both states keeps increasing.

In the midst of this thirsty-and-growing-thirstier area sits Yellowstone National Park and the larger Greater Yellowstone Ecosystem. With abundant water. Yellowstone contains more than 600 lakes and ponds and about 1,000 rivers and streams. The GYE contains the headwaters of seven great rivers.

Most of the water in Yellowstone and the GYE arrives as snow. The area's spring thaw quenches the thirst of much of the American West. But human-caused climate change now reduces snowpack and speeds up spring thaw. By late-summer the rivers run so low that maintaining a continuous water supply is difficult. Thus, the droughts.

All this makes me wonder when the next water-grabbing scheme generated by development around Yellowstone will hit. And if it does, will future backpackers still be able to wade through the Bechler?

27

Can Yellowstone Handle the Love?

———

As one of the last tour buses hisses and rumbles out of town, as Gardiner breathes a collective sigh of relief, as another summer of record-breaking visitation enters the books, I wonder about the impact all those visitors have on Yellowstone and its gateway towns. I'm not alone: other residents, local chambers of commerce, and Yellowstone officials worry about the strain that comes with all those visitors and their much-needed cash.

Like other gateway towns, Gardiner is surrounded by the mountains, forests, and rivers of the greater Yellowstone area. Attitudes toward such wildlands have changed dramatically over the years. Not so long ago, the land was coveted primarily as a place from which to take resources and create wealth. A few people got rich, most just got by. Then recreation and tourism—take only pictures; create only memories—boomed and brought millions of visitors eager to simply experience the area's wildlands and wildlife.

This greater Yellowstone area is classified by *The Atlas of Yellowstone* as a wildland complex: an area with a national park at its core, surrounded by Forest Service, Bureau of Land Management, or other public lands. National parks at the center of other wildland complexes include California's Yosemite, Arizona's Grand Canyon, Montana's Glacier, and Washington's North Cascades. Studies have shown that wildland complexes such as these stimulate economic growth and create wildland economies.

In the boom years of the late 1990s and early 2000s, for example, greater Yellowstone grew faster in terms of employment and population than rapidly growing areas such as Silicon Valley, Denver, and Seattle, according to *The Atlas of Yellowstone*. It came in second in terms of growth of per capita income. While that's impressive, I found even more striking a quote from one high-tech employer's recruitment page: "Why live in Silicon Valley when you can live in Paradise Valley?"

Choose greater Yellowstone's Paradise Valley over California's Silicon Valley? My, how times have changed. Greater Yellowstone's remote setting once scared businesses away. Now it attracts them and the entrepreneurs that create them. The area also attracts "amenity migrants," people—like many Gardiner residents I've met—who first choose where they want to live and then find or create work that pays for living there. Then there are newcomers who don't need to work at all: retirees lucky enough to live off of pensions and investments.

These visitors-turned-residents and the money they bring or jobs they create are one part of a wildland economy. Tourists—and their dollars—are another part. The more than four million visitors to Yellowstone in 2016 brought $524.3 million to communities near the park.

While gateway towns prosper from tourist dollars, they struggle with a huge problem: how to provide the services and infrastructure that those hordes of visitors need without bankrupting the small number of locals. Gardiner is a good example. With only about 850 year-round residents, the town services around 750,000 visitors each year.

Years ago, forward-thinking town leaders wondered where to get the money to support such visitation. They made Gardiner a Montana Resort Area District and implemented a resort tax. From June through September, the town collects a 3 percent tax on the things tourists want most: lodging, camping, food service, guides, and gifts. Those tax dollars help Gardiner pay for the things tourists need most: emergency services; water, sewer, and transportation improvements; and building and maintaining a visitor center. Over the next two decades the tax could generate up to $1 million each year, and the funds look secure since the number of visitors to Yellowstone keeps climbing.

While it took twenty-five years for the newly created Yellowstone National Park to reach the 10,000-visitor milestone, once cars entered the park, visitation soared. Cars and buses drove the need for road improvements. With improved roads, came more cars and buses; Yellowstone became a drive-thru park and a must-see. Steady growth in visitation continued with dips during the First World War, the Great Depression, and the Second World War. Then came a period of peace, prosperity, and packing the parks. Yellowstone hit one million annual visitors in 1948, two million in 1965, three million in 1992, and four million in 2015.

In September 2015, Park Superintendent Dan Wenk told the press, "We have been surprised by the size of the increase this year." By October as visitors kept coming, Wenk's surprise was tinged with concern, "We are delighted to see that more and more visitors are making their way to Yellowstone... However, it creates additional challenges for our staff who work hard to protect this amazing place while providing top-notch services for visitors. We want to do everything we can to make sure that park visitors have a safe and enjoyable trip, while at the same time protecting the special resources that Yellowstone was set aside to preserve."

One of the things the administration does is help to train the instructors, guides, and staff that work in the park. After a winter of recuperation from a frazzling summer of driving a bus in Yellowstone, Mary and I attended the NPS pre-summer training. Presenters covered a variety of topics, including wildlife, climate change, geology, and history. But the speakers that really opened my eyes were those who talked about the increase in visitation and its impact.

The first to comment was Deputy Superintendent Steve Iobst as he welcomed us to the training. He said a combination of three factors—more visitors, arriving in larger doses, and staying longer—have collided to tax the park's staff, infrastructure, landscape, and wildlife. And there's more to come. The park received great press as the star of the May 2016 issue of National Geographic—an issue that reached somewhere around forty million people. That publicity and the promotion of the 100th anniversary of the National Park Service should keep attendance high.

Since all visitors arrive in either tour buses or private vehicles, traffic has also increased. West Yellowstone, the gateway town with more visitors than any other, has been hardest hit, Iobst said. Sometimes the line of vehicles waiting to enter the park backed up all the way through West Yellowstone and out of town. And the delay didn't end for the excited, impatient, and sometimes frustrated tourists once they finally passed through the gate. Sometimes visitors had to endure a two-hour drive to cover the fourteen traffic-packed miles from the west entrance to Madison Junction.

People from many countries will be experiencing these traffic jams since more international visitors now make Yellowstone a destination. Linda Young, chief of Resource Education and Youth Programs, told us about Chinese visitors, since they make up the largest percentage of international tourists. For Chinese visitors, a trip to Yellowstone is expensive and may be a once-in-a-lifetime experience that few of their family and friends will ever have. That makes returning to China with photos of themselves in Yellowstone an essential part of their trip. This has led to such an increase in the use of selfie-sticks that the park newspaper now lists tips (in multiple languages) on how to take selfies safely. I think many visitors aren't reading the tips; last summer I was almost impaled on selfie-sticks numerous times.

Young said that the concept of "national park" is new to China, and national parks in China—which often have no backcountry—are quite different from Yellowstone. Chinese visitors arrive here believing that if there are trails, then they must not lead to a dangerous place. In Yellowstone, that's an incorrect and dangerous assumption. Also, wild animal shows are common in China, as is feeding wildlife. Being fined for feeding wildlife in Yellowstone may increase the cost of an already expensive visit.

And there's another, more intimate, cultural challenge. Young said that in China, people sit on the toilet in their home, but for sanitary reasons they place their feet on the toilet seat and squat over toilets in many public restrooms. Since roadside toilets in Yellowstone are very public, some Chinese visitors squat. Unfortunately, some miss the mark, and over time this creates messy and unsafe conditions. The problem is so widespread that park officials have slapped stickers on the doors of many restrooms. With images, the stickers communicate that sitting is allowed, squatting is not.

Another presenter told us about other impacts of Yellowstone's increasing visitation. Ryan Atwell, an NPS sociologist, recalled how the previous summer, during the heat of a record-breaking year, Superintendent Wenk asked him to help park administrators understand the range of change and ways to respond to increasing visitation.

Since then Atwell has travelled around the park interviewing staff—from rangers to concessionaires to 911 dispatchers. He has listened to first-hand accounts of how big crowds create even bigger challenges. As he described what he has found, I couldn't help but think that the picture he paints is one of a park under siege.

Yellowstone was simply not built to handle today's crowds. Atwell said that the park's infrastructure—the roads, parking lots, boardwalks, buildings, and bathrooms—is designed to handle about 2.5 million visitors a year, not 4 million.

The record-breaking 17 percent increase in visitors from 2014 to 2015 led to proportionally greater increases of certain problems, Atwell told us. The number of motor vehicle accidents with injury soared 167 percent. Instances of out-of-bounds camping (mostly tourists sleeping overnight in their cars) shot up 117 percent. The number of search and rescue events climbed 61 percent. The number of life flights increased 24 percent.

He summed up with the troubling observation that by mid-summer Yellowstone has almost all the issues of a mid-sized metropolitan area. This includes firearms, which are allowed in the park, but can't legally be fired. However, firearms were brandished five or six times in reaction to road rage.

Last summer, while driving the bus, I saw many situations that can lead to rage and acting out. Traffic crawls. Wildlife jams abound. Distracted driving is at an all-time high. Parking at popular attractions is scarce. Lines for refreshments are daunting. Delays at the other end of the digestive process are just as bad: in the heat of summer, lines of twenty to forty visitors at bathrooms are common. Park officials fear that problems such as these may lead to other unsettling changes in visitor behavior. Atwell has heard reports of theft and poaching, damage to thermal features, and trampling of vegetation.

As administrators begin to understand the incredible range of problems caused by record visitation, they struggle to find solutions. Atwell shared a few with us. For the short term, administrators have "overhired" NPS staff by 5 percent and will place extra staff at critical or crowded places. One mid-range solution would be to increase tour bus education and accountability. An example of this surfaced at a different NPS training when attendees complained about tour bus drivers that sent their passengers into roadside forests with toilet paper when the bathrooms were crowded and waiting for the crowd to disperse would put the drivers behind schedule. A long-term solution to overcrowding, Atwell emphasized, will NOT be more facilities. More beds, campgrounds, and roads would just increase the number of visitors.

As I sat in the training remembering my tussles with crowding in the park last summer and the crowds already evident before Memorial Day of this year, I found myself visualizing Yellowstone at a tipping point. No one I have spoken to expects visitation to decrease. That means staff and administrators will have to devise ways to accommodate crowds and preserve the park. This won't be quick or easy, especially with chronic funding shortages.

Each attendee to the NPS training received a copy of that National Geographic issue featuring Yellowstone. As I browsed through mine during a break, I came upon a quote

Superintendent Wenk made regarding the increase in the number of park visitors and the challenge facing Yellowstone: "I believe we are rapidly coming to a point where one of two things is going to happen. Either we as a society agree to limit the number of visitors in order to protect resources that are incredibly sensitive to disturbance or we allow the numbers to go unchecked—knowing that we are diminishing, perhaps irreparably, the very things that attract people worldwide to this one-of-a-kind national park."

In the time I've spent with groups of visitors to Yellowstone, I have seen how deeply most love this park. They call this place magical, declare that a visit here can be life-changing. And when considering each visitor's experience, I can't think of a better outcome. But when we subject this park to four million or more of those loving visitors, I don't see how Yellowstone can handle that much love.

28

Reserve Your Park

———

While researching this book, I talked to people who have studied the challenges facing Yellowstone. Most agreed that overuse is a critical issue. And that someone, somewhere has to draw a line, cap attendance, and say, "Enough!" Yet visitation keeps rising.

Why can't Yellowstone's superintendent just limit the number of cars or buses or people that come into the park? According to one knowledgeable person, the NPS party line seems to be, "You can't cap attendance because someone will scream." That someone might be a senator or representative that could reduce the already meager park funding.

Besides, that person added, overuse is not a problem that a superintendent here or there can solve; overuse is systemwide. Yosemite, Zion, Arches, and Glacier have all tried and failed to solve the problem of too many tourists and vehicles. A solution will have to come from higher up the NPS military-style chain of command.

One possible systemwide solution that I heard about from a retired Yellowstone administrator involves the ten most popular parks in the nation agreeing on a way to reduce or cap visitation. This would require the cooperation of all ten superintendents. It would require the support of the Department of the Interior and possibly the president of the United States. It would require the support of influential organizations and individuals. That's a lot of people to get on the same unpopular page. No wonder attendance keeps rising.

Yellowstone's management has explored the overuse issue. They brought Swiss experts in to look at light rail as a solution to traffic. Won't work. Other advisors recommended an electric train from West Yellowstone. Too expensive. Some call for widening roads or building parking lots or even parking garages. Results in more people and overuse.

The more I asked questions and listened to answers, the more I started to see overuse as a problem that will just go on and on with no relief in sight. If that's true, then I wonder when—not if—some part of Yellowstone's admittedly aging, overtaxed, and minimally maintained infrastructure will fail. That retired administrator foresees a ten- to fifteen-year window before catastrophe strikes. Maybe a boardwalk collapses and people are burned or killed in a thermal feature. Maybe an overpass or bridge fails and visitors in vehicles are injured or killed. A terrible accident that occurred because the facility has been overused would create such an uproar that change might come.

The problem is not just with the unwillingness of the National Park Service, Department of the Interior, and the president to take an unpopular stand and limit attendance.

Other powerful parties want to see even more people in the parks. One significant source of this pressure was described by John Lemons, a professor of biological and environmental science, in his article entitled *Splendid No More*. "By the 1970s, most parks had concessions owned by some of the largest US corporations, which were steadfast in encouraging use and development in the parks. There are now more than 500 active concession contracts to provide services in national parks, which gross more than $1 billion annually."

That's a lot of money and careers at stake and these concessionaires want more—not less—development of national parks. "Unfortunately," writes Lemons, "most of the development in parks has occurred in the most scenic and significant conservation areas."

Lemons cites the battle in Yosemite in 1980 as one example of how powerful forces rail against restricting attendance and fight for more development. When Yosemite's General Management Plan recommended reducing car-accessible campsites by 60 percent and parking by 75 percent, one opposition group cried, "What they're doing is nothing less than stealing a national park from the people." None of the plan's proposals for reducing cars in Yosemite Valley were implemented.

I looked at Yosemite's visitor statistics, which show 2.4 million visitors in 1980. Within twenty-five years that number had swelled to 4.1 million. That's a lot of additional profit from extra hotel rooms, gasoline, milkshakes, and cool t-shirts sold by concessionaires.

Lemons concludes: "If national parks are truly to be the 'crown jewels' of a nation's scenery, plants and wildlife, the NPS must develop a visionary policy to guide the management of its parks. Parks cannot be all things to all people; if the NPS is to err, it ought to favour conservation of scenery and wildlife at the expense of use."

Even if the Park Service isn't willing to limit visitation, why not at least stop promoting it? Though many parks are overcrowded, the Park Service recently launched their multi-year "Find Your Park" promotion, the largest marketing campaign in the history of our national parks. They designed the promotion to bring more people—mainly millennials and urban dwellers—to the parks. The influence of large corporations is evident: sponsors of the campaign include Subaru, REI, American Express, Disney, and others that figure to profit from more travelers. The promotion worked well and was one cause of Yellowstone's overuse.

I think that this ill-advised promotion can teach the NPS a way to reduce visitation as well. I encourage the Park Service to run a different multi-year campaign. This new campaign would encourage people that have found their park to now "Reserve Your Park." Here's how it might work.

Each day in Yellowstone the number of people who stay overnight in the park is already limited by the number of hotel beds and campsites. If park administration also capped the number of day-trippers, they could reduce park visitation each and every day. Daily attendance would be controlled so that at the end of the year, total visitation would be within the range the park can handle—say, three million visitors instead of four million. A portion of the hotel, campground, and day use permits could be reserved in advance. The remainder of the day's slots would be available for people who arrive that day. But once that day's maximum number is reached no one can enter the park until someone leaves.

When I presented this admittedly simplistic idea to that retired Yellowstone administrator, the immediate reply was, "Can't you just see an irate visitor screaming, 'I drove two days to get here and now you won't let me in? That's crazy. This is my park! I'm calling my senator!'"

Yes, I admitted, I can imagine that. But if a Reserve Your Park promotion educates people that Yellowstone and other parks are at risk from overuse, that visitation must be controlled, and that reservations are best, then potential visitors could plan accordingly. A family that could not get a reservation for July 4, for example, might get one for July 15.

Oh, I was told, that's good in theory, but what if the breadwinner can only get off for the week of July 4 and can't get July 15?

Well, I countered, then they could enjoy another national park that has space available. There are, after all, more than 400 units in the National Park System, including fifty-eight other national parks. Many are not overused.

This spirited discussion made me wonder how other popular resources limit attendance. I found that the Bureau of Land Management has a lottery-based reservation system to visit The Wave, a sandstone rock formation in Arizona. Reservations are required—sometimes months ahead—for backcountry camping in Yellowstone and many other national parks. When full, the Alaska State Ferry sends travelers scurrying for other transportation. Even Disneyland has to turn guests away.

I agree that using a Reserve Your Park campaign or any other tool that limits attendance will create a long list of unhappy people. At the top of that list will be the hopefuls unable to get a reservation or enter the park on the day they arrive. Local, state, and national politicians will find themselves forced to listen to these angry citizens. Park administrators will hear from the politicians and watch receipts fall at the entrance gates. Park concessionaires will worry about their careers and profits because fewer visitors means fewer buyers. Tour bus companies will have to park some empty buses. Businesses in Gardiner and other gateway towns will feel the bite too.

But regardless of how many people are unhappy at first, limiting attendance in Yellowstone—and other overused parks—can protect these precious resources. And in the end, protection must be the deciding factor.

29

Fool's Gold

———

Though only six miles by gravel road from Gardiner, still snowless in early October, snow covers the grounds of Hell's A-Roarin' Outfitters. Structures abound: a huge barn, lots of smaller outbuildings, plenty of horse corrals, and a large log lodge. All nestle among tall conifers and share a breathtaking view of Gardiner Basin and Electric Peak.

Nathan Varley and I drove up the mountain to Hell's A-Roarin' to tour the area around the nearby, proposed, and controversial Crevice Mine. We were invited as Gardiner residents and members of the Bear Creek Council. The Greater Yellowstone Coalition (GYC), a regional organization devoted to protecting the Yellowstone area, organized the tour in partnership with the Yellowstone Gateway Business Coalition.

As Nathan and I walk toward the lodge, a fit and friendly retriever with a well-chewed toy in its mouth greets us. Though we are running a little late, I can't resist stopping to pet and play. When we reach the lodge, Sue Johnson greets us and ushers us into what she and her husband Warren

Johnson call their trophy room. The large room has a ceiling high enough that the murmurs of those already gathered here echo. A massive stone fireplace, fire blazing, fills one corner of the room. Warren Johnson says with pride that he collected every rock in that fireplace, and each reminds him of a particular moment. I appreciate his sentiment.

I appreciate much less the trophies that fill the room. Mounted heads from a variety of animals hang on every wall. In addition to the heads, there are full-bodied trophies including a grizzly bear that reminds me of my vision of the hunter and the fearless bear. There's also a full-bodied black bear, moose, and bighorn sheep. Some of the taxidermy captures action. A mountain lion and mountain goats climb the rocks of the fireplace. Another mountain lion is frozen in time attacking a deer. But my heart sinks when I spot a wolf howling forever at the ceiling. I assume it strayed from the protection of Yellowstone National Park, about a half mile from the lodge.

Standing there, I wonder what I—a wildlife advocate—am doing in a room stuffed with wildlife trophies. I remind myself that I'm here to help stop the proposed gold mine. The Johnsons—like everyone else in their trophy room—are also against that mine. Regardless of how much I dislike trophies, the Johnsons and I are on the same team.

Others present include representatives from the offices of two of Montana's three U.S. congressional representatives, a Park County commissioner and his opponent in the upcoming election, the director of the Park County Environmental Council, a geologist, a geophysicist, an NPS employee representing Yellowstone, and a couple GYC staff. Reporters have come from a newspaper and a TV station to cover the tour.

It's not hard to fill a room with people opposed to the idea of mining right on the border of Yellowstone. In fact, the only person I've met who wants the mine is Michael Werner, the managing partner of Crevice Mining Group, LLC, the company that would operate the mine if it's approved by the Montana Department of Environmental Quality (MDEQ).

Werner is not here today, but I heard him speak a few months ago at a meeting he arranged at the Gardiner Community Center. He wanted to convince locals that the mine would be good for Gardiner and good for him. His message was interrupted by angry comments and fell on deaf ears.

Today's meeting begins when Warren Johnson introduces himself to the group. He leans against a bar that has an ornate mirror behind it and could have enhanced the set of a western movie. His Stetson hat completes the image. The rest of us—wearing baseball caps and wool hats—stand in a horseshoe around the bar. Johnson says that he and Sue leased this place in 1982 and bought it three years later. They have earned a living here working as outfitters, guiding people on excursions to hunt and fish, ride and hike.

Joe Josephson, organizer of the event for GYC, invites questions. I tell the group that Michael Werner assured us at the community meeting that his mine won't affect wildlife because there's not much wildlife in the area. I ask Johnson what he thinks of Werner's assessment.

"That's nonsense," he says with a frown. He explains that he hunts around this lodge and the proposed Crevice Mine. He's found that elk use the area as a corridor to and from Yellowstone. So do deer, grizzly bear, and a growing number of moose. (Though some of them now line this room, I think to myself.)

Steve Koehler, a geologist standing beside me, also has something to say about Werner and the community meeting. Koehler has more than twenty-six years experience in gold exploration. He and his wife are Gardiner residents; she works in Yellowstone. Koehler tells Johnson that when Werner presented his proposal in Gardiner, "There was nothing about community involvement or how can we help you and how can we embrace this together and build trust." Koehler said that this is the opposite of what he expected from Werner and the opposite of how the company Koehler works for interacts with communities where they want to explore for gold.

Marty Malone, a Park County commissioner, remembers when a previous mining company came in and took a more inclusive approach. They joined local clubs, went to community meetings, spoke to environmental groups. They described their plan and asked for input. Malone has not seen Werner and Crevice Mining Group do this. Instead, Werner wants to know what Park County can do for him and his company.

Geophysicist Dave Chambers speaks next. He is founder and president of a non-profit that provides technical assistance on mining and water quality to public interest groups (including GYC) and tribal governments. He says that Kinross Gold Corp., an international mining company, could mine in this area but has chosen not to in part because locals do not want a mine on the border of Yellowstone.

Brett French, the newspaper reporter, pen in one hand, reporter's notebook in the other, asks Johnson, "How would the mine affect your business here?"

Johnson points out that he has no nearby neighbors and that helps his business as an outfitter. He fears that the sight of the mine's big dump trucks going up and down the road and the noise they would create "could harm our business tremendously."

The trucks he dreads were discussed at Werner's earlier meeting. Each powerful truck will pull a long trailer and a shorter one. Werner told us that the mine will run ten trucks daily, day and night, 350 days a year. Someone asked if he would be willing to modify the schedule so that the noisy machines would not travel at night when residents are trying to sleep in Gardiner and Jardine, the community closest to the mine. Werner said he would not.

Josephson brings to a close this first stop on the tour and asks us to meet in the parking lot. When Nathan and I walk outside, the retriever, with a different toy in its mouth, greets us like an old friend. As I squat and smile and pull on the toy, I see the road runs right by the lodge. The smile collapses to a scowl as I imagine how those hulking trucks, with engines growling, gears grinding, and brakes hissing will shatter this tranquil scene.

Our next stop on the tour is Crevice Mountain Lodge, another endangered business. The lodge sits at 8,200 feet, just below the peak of Crevice Mountain. We will get there in all-wheel drive vehicles. I give the retriever one final pat and jump into the last car leaving. As we bounce up the rough, rutted road that climbs to the lodge, I can't imagine one of those huge trucks navigating this road. Or, worse yet, coming towards me as I drive.

When we gather outside of the historic guest ranch, a gregarious cat by the name of Smokey greets us with abundant purrs and rubs. Cheryl Standish, her cheeks red from the cold, stands in front of her lodge, a single-story log cabin with moose antlers hanging above the door, firewood stacked on the large porch, and fresh snow dusting wooden Adirondack chairs. She tells us that Crevice Mountain Lodge has been part of her life for fifty years, since she was twelve years old. Her outfitter parents built the lodge and started the business.

French asks her, "How do you feel about a mine being proposed in your backyard?"

"I have a few concerns," Standish says in a tone that hints at her opposition to the mine. One worry is for her water supply. She explains that it's hard to find water on a mountain top. If Werner, while exploring for gold nearby, drills the proposed 150 holes that are each 500 feet deep, rocks below ground may crack, "If that rock cracks, you don't know where the water's going to go. So I might lose my well."

Her second concern is that the sight and sound of the trucks running day and night "will hurt my business because people come here for a getaway."

"What does this place mean to you?" French asks.

"It's mostly my livelihood," she replies with a smile, "but I love it."

"Why's that?"

"I think I like to get away from the soap opera of life." She pauses for a moment and adds, "When people come here, there are a lot of little kids that have never seen the Milky Way. They've never let a chicken out in the morning or put one in at night." Those kids come to her lodge for a week with their family and don't care that there's no TV or games, she adds.

Josephson thanks Standish then distributes maps and tells us that we will now walk along a two-track road, through a gate, onto US Forest Service land, and into one of the potential mining areas. As Josephson leads the way, Smokey the cat tags along.

Our first stop is just a short walk to a fence that separates Standish's land from US Forest Service land. Josephson points to a snow-covered meadow bordered by conifers. He says that this is where the mine's main pile of waste rock will grow. The pile will bump against the fence and be very close to the lodge where people come to get away from life's hustle and bustle. This lack of buffer between Werner's operation and nearby private land was one of the problems MDEQ had with his application.

Werner has applied twice for permission to explore for gold here. Both applications have been returned by MDEQ with lengthy letters citing problems that Crevice Mining Group must address. Werner has said he will reapply.

Chambers believes that the rock pile will be much larger than Werner estimates. Whatever the size, it will be visible for a very long time. Centuries will creep by before vegetation covers the pile; waste rock is not good growth material. This gentle meadow will become an industrial dump.

Chambers next explains that mining for gold produces two byproducts: waste rock with little or no gold and ore that may contain a worthwhile amount of gold. He says that miners typically extract the gold on site by grinding the ore to a fine powder and mixing in cyanide. Once the gold is extracted, the processed ore—now called tailings—remains on site permanently.

Tailings, we learn, are a problem waiting to happen. Chambers explains that tailings can produce toxic liquid waste that can leach into and contaminate streams and wells. He turns and points toward the park and the Yellowstone River adding, "Anything that leaches is going to go downhill toward the park." If this occurs, it could be difficult to stop, and that chore would fall to the mining company.

If toxic liquid from Crevice Mine contaminated the Yellowstone River, the wildland economy of Park County would suffer financially. This summer, the river was closed for recreation due to a massive fish die-off blamed on poor water conditions. In just weeks, Park County businesses lost between $360,000 and $524,000 when visitors decided to stay away, according to one study.

Toxic waste is just one environmental nightmare with gold mining. A company applying to mine must describe how it will monitor for environmental problems. Another reason that MDEQ returned the Crevice Mining Group's application was because it did not adequately address monitoring.

One way to avoid dangerous piles of tailings here is to haul the ore to an off-site processor elsewhere. At the community meeting, Werner said that he would process off-site, truck the ore as needed, regardless of distance.

But Chambers doubts that hauling ore to a distant processor would be economically feasible. Besides, he says, the most likely processor is "talking about shutting down in a year." Trucking ore a couple of miles to Jardine for processing would be Werner's more likely and most affordable option. Josephson reveals that Werner has already staked a couple of claims that could be used for milling ore on public land in Jardine.

If Werner is able to advance from exploration to full-scale mining, Chambers explains, the waste rock pile in this meadow would expand from covering less than ten acres to burying a couple hundred acres. The pile could grow up to 100 feet high.

Standish, who has joined us on the tour and now cradles Smokey, says she went to Yellowstone the other day, and as she walked across the Hellroaring Plateau she could see this meadow, this future waste rock dump. From where we stand, we see cars driving in Yellowstone. At Werner's community meeting, he assured us that his operation would not be visible from Yellowstone. But, if we can see cars from here, Werner's huge trucks and ugly waste pile will surely be visible from there—and detract from the view that visitors from around the world have come to admire.

Josephson moves us along to the next stop. We gather near what's called an adit, a hole in the ground that was an entrance to a mine. Miners worked this area starting in the late 1800s, but the last commercial mine closed in the late 1900s. Today, some Gardiner residents say they miss those good-paying mining jobs.

At the community meeting, Werner said his mine will generate forty-four jobs. But the few high-paying jobs require skills so specialized that filling them with Gardiner residents is unlikely. Locals would probably do the laborer jobs that pay $22 per hour, Werner said. A woman stood up and announced with a hint of contempt, "I earn that much waiting tables."

She's not alone in downplaying Werner's imagined jobs. More than 200 local businesses have joined the Yellowstone Gateway Business Coalition and oppose the mine, regardless of the jobs it might create in this wildland economy. Members of the coalition have travelled to Washington, D.C. to lobby against the mine.

After we look at the adit, Chambers and Koehler discuss the economics of gold mining. Koehler picks up a rock and holds it out to the group. He explains that this is quartz and may contain gold. Cameras click. No matter how hidden, gold excites.

At a previous mine in this area where Werner was chief operating officer, the company removed one-quarter to one-half ounce of gold from each ton of rock. Though that sounds tiny, Koehler says that's a pretty good return.

Demand drives a company to move so much rock for so little gold, and technology creates that demand. Koehler smiles widely and says, "I've got a few crowns in my mouth that are made of gold." Then he reaches into his pocket, pulls out his phone, and asks, "How many people have a smart phone? You own gold. Gold is a huge part of the technological revolution that we're in right now." Gold is used in camera bodies and lenses, TVs, stereos, vehicles, even cancer treatments.

Mining companies exist to satisfy that demand at a profit. But doing so is far from guaranteed. The price at which gold sells fluctuates. A few years ago, gold hit an all-time high of slightly over $1,900 per ounce but has been falling since. The day before the tour the price fell by $48 to $1,275 per ounce.

Finding and mining gold to sell at any price is a challenge. "The easy gold deposits around the planet," says Koehler, "have been found and exploited." Scarcity drives up costs. Reputable mining companies calculate what is called the "all-in sustaining cost." This includes every expense associated with producing each ounce of gold. A few years ago, that cost was as much as $1,100 per ounce.

When gold sold for $1,900 per ounce and cost $1,100 to extract, profits soared. But at today's selling price of $1,275 per ounce, Koehler says, there's precious little money to be made. And worse yet, little money to be spent addressing inevitable environmental predicaments.

The combination of too little gold and too many expenses leads straight to bankruptcy, a common event in the gold mining industry. Chambers says that most of the companies that have gone bankrupt have been bonded, but the bonds haven't been large enough to cover cleanup costs. Numerous private mining companies have crept away and left the public with a bill for millions of dollars to clean up their mess.

"Who is the watchdog to make sure that the mining is done correctly?" I ask Chambers.

He says that if Werner mines on Forest Service land, then the Forest Service would be the watchdog. When I ask if the Forest Service has the funds to do a good job, a cynical laugh ripples through the crowd. Chambers says that the Forest Service claims to have learned from its mistakes and is now better at monitoring. Then he adds, "When gold prices drop down to below $1,000 per ounce again, we'll see some bankruptcies." Who will pay for the mess that bankrupt gold diggers leave behind?

Koehler points out that the mining industry is being held to a higher standard today because of past failures. He says that with Yellowstone next door, a mining company must do even better. "But what I've seen proposed up here is a little bit frightening to me." He has read Crevice Mining Group's application and finds it "littered with dozens of red flags."

As Josephson moves us along to the last stop on the walking tour, Smokey follows. When we stop on the rutted

Forest Service road, the cat rubs against my leg. Smokey knows how to prospect for strokes, and I give them.

Off to our right, Blacktail Deer Plateau is obvious in the distance. The Yellowstone River borders the plateau and reflects the morning sun. Josephson points to a stand of aspen trees, bright yellow in fall. They are close, only about 1,000 feet away and on the border of Yellowstone. He tells us that Crevice Mining Group would mine beneath the ground we stand on. That would create an unknown number of surface disturbances right here, more mess to view from the park.

Bill Berg, candidate for Park County commissioner, asks the question that has been on my mind and probably everyone else's as well. "Other than lack of funding and incompetence, what would stop him from proceeding?"

Koehler explains that Werner holds leases to private property, and we are limited in what we can do to stop him, especially if he gets permission to explore. So commenting on the exploration application during any MDEQ comment period is essential. During the last period, Nathan, as chair of Bear Creek Council, sent a long letter outlining the council's concerns. About 200 other people and organizations commented to MDEQ as well. An online petition against the mine collected 73,000 signatures.

Lack of financing could stop the mine since holes in the ground swallow money. Koehler says that a company may spend millions or tens of millions of dollars before extracting a single ounce of gold. He should know since budgeting for exploration is part of his job. He has noticed that some of the items missing in Crevice Mining Group's application are those that cost a lot. "I don't think they allocated enough money to the exploration program that they outlined with DEQ. They're way under budget."

The good news, then, is that Crevice Mining Group could run out of money and abandon the project early on, before they do much damage. The bad news is that inadequate funding is a serious concern due to the cost of monitoring and mitigating environmental issues.

"Does MDEQ assess financial ability?" Berg asks.

Koehler and Chambers agree that MDEQ does not assess a company's financial ability when reviewing its application to explore for gold. Neither does the Forest Service.

On that disturbing note, we turn and head back down the road toward our cars and a hot lunch awaiting us in the trophy room at Hell's A-Roarin'. I'm looking forward to seeing the retriever but not the trophies. As we pass the future waste dump, Koehler says, "That waste rock pile is on a steep slope. We're in an earthquake zone up here. That kind of sends chills up my spine."

The vision of Werner and his Crevice Mining Group digging here chills me too. I'm concerned about the discrepancies between what Werner told us locals at the community meeting and what I heard today. I'm concerned that his application to explore has been sent back twice with problems. I'm concerned about his company's ability to monitor and fix environmental problems. And I'm concerned that Werner may not have the financial backing to pay for a clean-up or survive a drop in the price of gold. The company may claim bankruptcy and leave a mess for the public to clean up. All within sight of Yellowstone National Park and leaching distance of the Yellowstone River.

———

As this book went to production, Mary and I attended a meeting at Chico Hot Springs in Paradise Valley, just north of Gardiner. The large room was filled to standing-room only. A row of TV cameras and still photographers lined the back of the room.

We sat with a number of other Gardiner residents. All of us had been invited to hear Sally Jewell, then secretary of the interior, give good news. She announced that the Department of the Interior had decided to make off limits for two years the public lands surrounding the private lands that Crevice Mining Group wants to mine. The public lands around Chico Hot Springs that another company wants to mine were also put off limits. This action gives everyone time to study this issue and the impact of mining, she told us.

In addition to Jewell, other officials spoke: Robert Bonnie, an under secretary in the U.S. Department of Agriculture; Steve Bullock, Montana's recently reelected governor; U.S. Senator Jon Testor; and Park County Commissioner Steve Caldwell. Each applauded the decision and said that this action by the Department of the Interior resulted from the incredible efforts made locally. They thanked all of us smiling and clapping and hooting locals for organizing and voicing our concerns. They also warned that this battle is far from over. No one knows what will happen with a new president and new secretary of the interior. No one knows what might happen with legal challenges to setting the public land aside.

I talked with many locals before, during, and after the announcement. All are committed to continuing the fight against gold mining near Yellowstone National Park. As a number of speakers said that day, "Yellowstone is more valuable than gold."

30

Food for the Masses

Ours is the only car on the side of the road that runs between Mammoth Hot Springs and Norris Geyser Basin. I turn off the headlights and cut the engine. The sun is not yet up, and as our eyes adjust to the low light, Mary and I can just make out the meadow where we watched a big male grizzly feed on a carcass yesterday. Brimming with anticipation of seeing the grizzly or wolves or who knows what else on the carcass today, we peer into mysterious shades of black and gray. Silent moments pass; daylight increases. The tops of meadow-edge conifers become jagged silhouettes that pierce the brightening sky of this late-October day.

Headlights and taillights of cars arriving and parking on both sides of the road prove that although most visitors have left the park for the year, hardcore wildlife watchers have not. Like us, they are here this morning because they know that in a few days this road and most of Yellowstone's Grand Loop will be behind locked gates, inaccessible to cars and waiting to be buried under snow. The wildlands and wildlife will have a respite from humans until spring.

As the morning light increases, Mary can scan with binoculars and spots two shadows moving near where the bear had fed yesterday. "Female elk," she whispers. "Their heads are up. They're way alert." Her head swivels to track the elk as they hurry away. When they disappear behind a hummock, she scans back to the meadow and exclaims, "There's the bear! He's walking through the grass."

I grab my camera and aiming past Mary's shoulder, zoom in on the meadow. But there's still not enough light for the camera to be useful. I drop the camera in my lap and wait for her update.

Mary whispers that the bear is heading out of the meadow and into the darkness below the conifers. Then, with obvious disappointment, "He's gone. I can't see him." She tosses the binoculars on the dashboard, glances at me, turns back to her window, and sighs. "I wish some ravens would fly in to show us exactly where that carcass is."

Less than a minute later she exclaims, "Oh, my gosh, there are four ravens flying in." As they land in the top of a conifer, she pleads, "Come on. Show me. Show me."

We laugh and relax. Nothing beats ravens for finding carcasses and attracting wolves. Maybe today a pack will come to claim any remains of the carcass the bear leaves.

We figure that the carcass is an elk the grizzly poached from wolves. Bears are not fast enough to chase and bring down a healthy adult elk, though there are reports of a few grizzlies taking down adult elk with sneak attacks. But wolves bring down lots of elk and provide plenty of meals for opportunistic bears to commandeer in spring, summer, and fall. The exchange is simple: If a grizzly wants a wolf kill, the grizzly takes a wolf kill. That's probably what happened here, based on what we saw yesterday.

Yesterday morning, about a mile north of where we now sit, we enjoyed watching a lone black wolf bound through a meadow dusted with frost. As it trotted in the direction of Bunsen Peak, it stopped several times to howl. Mesmerized, we listened to a pack's reply from the southeast. After the black wolf disappeared from our view, we turned around and watched a group of fifteen elk, males and females, young and old. Painted golden in the low morning sun, they grazed on the move.

Once the elk left, we drove until we came upon this meadow and the feeding grizzly. We calculated the distance we had driven from the black wolf and realized that the responding howls we had heard may have come from a pack that had lost their elk kill to the bear.

After yesterday's spectacular sunrise, we watched the grizzly with our naked eyes and optics. He was about 150 yards from the road. He ate, stopped, stood up, looked around, sniffed the air. At one point, he stared at us and yawned. Through the spotting scope, we could see blood on his long, pointed canine teeth. Over the next two hours, he never strayed more than a few yards from his meal.

An elk is a large and easily digestible meal for a grizzly. But grizzlies are omnivores, and meat makes up only about a third of their diet. The other two-thirds comes from more than 250 species of plants, according to *Yellowstone Resources and Issues*. They devour grass, dandelions, berries, roots, truffles, mushrooms, and white bark pine nuts. They munch ants and army cutworm moths. They ravage food caches of pocket gophers and squirrels. They snatch and gobble fish. And they steal kills from wolves.

Since late summer, this big bear has been in the throes of hyperphagia, driven to devour as much food as possible before disappearing into his den. Adding fat that he will survive off of all winter is all that matters. During this phase, he may go for days without sleeping, which takes a back seat to eating. He may gain as much as three pounds in one day; ninety in a month.

But that food-obsessed bear isn't the only animal that needs to eat. To see who else would come to dine, we returned today—along with many other hopefuls—to his roadside feeding area. We are excited to watch how the grizzly handles the hungry ravens, magpies, eagles, and coyotes that may come to scavenge.

Mary grabs the binoculars from the dashboard where she had tossed them. She zooms in on one of the four ravens that landed in the conifer. She searches the tree and then where other trees meet the meadow. Her head stops, and she says, "Yes! There's a coyote coming in."

As she hands me the binoculars, we giggle in anticipation— we love watching coyotes, those intelligent tricksters. I raise the binoculars to my eyes: the tall, golden grasses below a conifer spread and the coyote's beautiful reddish-brown and gray head appears. The coyote pauses, ears straight up, eyes wide open and locked on us. It stands frozen as if debating whether to proceed. Then it pads toward a raven that has dropped from the conifer to peck at what must be scraps in the grass.

Mary opens her door, grabs the spotting scope, and scrambles down the roadside bank. I join her, and we watch as more ravens land in the tree or on the ground. Soon the coyote is joined by another, probably its mate since neither is posturing—angling its head, baring its teeth, arching its back—to decide who claims the meal. A couple of magpies fly in, land on the ground amidst the ravens, and hop here and there, pecking.

Mary, eye glued to the scope, whispers, "Whoa, there's the bear. He's back and coming out of the woods and heading toward the coyotes."

For a better view of what will happen next, she shoulders the scope and scurries about twenty yards up the road. I follow her past parked cars and excited people brandishing scopes and cameras.

While that bear feels driven to find food, we visitors are just as driven to watch him before he—and all the rest of the grizzlies—disappear for winter. Almost all of Yellowstone's 150 to 200 grizzlies will have denned by the first week of December. If food remains plentiful, thanks to the return of wolves, they may stay out a little longer.

To prepare his winter den, this big guy may take a week to excavate up to a ton of dirt and rocks using his big paws and long claws. Once finished, he may chew off spruce or fir boughs, drag them inside the den, and build a thick, insulating nest to curl into. Falling snow will eventually cover the den's entrance, add more insulation, and dim the lights. Time to sleep.

During a hibernation of four months or so, he will not eat, drink, defecate, or urinate. And his body will change. His temperature may drop twelve degrees. His respiration will slow from about ten breaths per minute to one per minute. His heart rate will fall from around fifty beats per minute to less than half of that. While he may lose almost a third of his body weight, he will maintain muscle mass.

From the roadside, Mary, with the spotting scope, and I, with the camera's telephoto, watch spellbound as one of the two coyotes walks through the increasing number of ravens and magpies and stops within a couple of feet of the feeding bear's big head, with all those sharp teeth. This seems brazen, but perhaps a careful coyote—like a watchful wolf—has little to fear, since a bear isn't quick enough to catch either. As Doug Smith and Gary Ferguson write in *Decade of the Wolf,* "For the most part wolves are to bears what mosquitoes might be to the rest of us—pesky annoyances."

The coyote stares at the bear, perhaps using what it sees, hears, and smells to assess the grizzly's temperament. Satisfied, it sidles up to the carcass, bites into the meat, jerks its head from side to side, rips a chunk away, and starts chewing. The bear, just on the other side of the carcass, doesn't appear to notice.

But he does glance to his rear at the second coyote that is busy scrounging scraps. Then he turns back to the carcass, takes another bite, and, without warning, lunges at the rear coyote. It sprints away, eyes wide, tail between its legs. The other coyote, though not charged, hustles away as well. The grizzly returns to the carcass and resumes eating. And in a few moments so do the two coyotes, unfazed, unharmed, and as yet unfulfilled.

While the coyotes and grizzly posture over who eats what, another raven lands on the branches of a dead and downed tree just behind the bear. It observes for a moment and then flutters to the ground, amid a writhing mass of magpies and ravens. It pecks and pulls and takes flight, a strip of meat dangling from its beak as it heads for a cache site. Another raven alights, takes the departing raven's place, and startles two magpies that flutter a couple of feet above the orgy, land on the other side of the carcass, and resume eating. The bear lunges at the birds and all take flight, circling above the carcass. This bear knows that ravens and magpies can rob him of hundreds of pounds of meat. When he continues feeding, the hungry birds return, one by one.

For two hours we marvel at how a bear, two coyotes, and many ravens and magpies share what noted Yellowstone biologist John Varley once called food for the masses.

———

A few days later, after the grizzly, coyotes, ravens, magpies, and bear watchers are gone, park rangers removed the signs that kept visitors away from the bear's feeding area. Since then Mary and I have crossed the meadow on three different days to study up close the site that we spent hours observing from afar.

Now on our last visit, we find wolf scat on a trail near the grizzly's feeding area. Not far from the scat, we come upon countless clumps of hair scattered between knee-high sagebrush. The strands are about two inches long, the top portion elk-tan, the rest white. We guess that the wolves brought the elk down in this spot.

The only other remnant of the elk we find is a lower jaw bone, small with teeth intact. Since the teeth show almost no wear, we surmise that the meal was a young elk, perhaps from that group of fifteen we first saw near the lone black wolf. Only the elk, the bear, and maybe some wolves know what actually took place.

In the bear's feeding area, we find that just in front of the downed tree where the raven had perched is a ten-foot by twenty-five-foot area that looks like a garden plot ready for fall planting. The grasses are gone, the soil is turned. Two small depressions have been dug. Along the edges of this grizzly dining room lie many piles of bear and coyote scat.

Standing where the bear once stood, I can see the road, which seems close. A car speeds by, followed by a rental RV. I hear their engines and the hum of their tires on pavement. I'm sure that the bear could also have heard the chatter and chuckling of all his watchers. With his superior sense of smell, he would have caught the stench of exhaust fumes, after shave, perfume, and sun screen. Yet with all that human presence, he did not drag the carcass into the forest to a more secluded, more protected, spot. He did not seem afraid of all the humans.

Then I picture this bear on another carcass, near another road, but outside of Yellowstone and no longer protected by the Endangered Species Act. Driven again by hyperphagia, he has travelled many miles in search of food and poached another carcass from wolves. The bear is eating. He hears a pickup truck and watches it crunch to a stop on the side of the road.

A man climbs out, walks to the front of the truck, and rests his elbows on the hood. He looks through a scope. Not a spotting scope. The scope of a powerful rifle.

The bear looks at the man but makes no effort to flee. He's seen plenty of humans act like this before, and he has never been harmed. Curious, he stands and yawns, exposing his chest to the man.

Leaning into the truck, the man nestles the stock of the rifle into his shoulder. He peers into the scope and exhales a long quiet breath. Ever so gently, he squeezes the trigger.

The bear feels the sharp pain of a bullet ripping into his chest. He falls to the ground, his blood mixing with that of the carcass he was eating only seconds earlier. He twists and writhes and exhales his last breath.

The man, rifle at the ready, marches toward the motionless animal, excited to take his trophy home. He imagines the bear's head on the wall, a trophy of pride. He visualizes the brown coat with silver highlights on the floor near his fireplace.

This troubling vision makes me sad for the bear and angry at the shooter. But another, more painful thought, enters my mind. Mary and I and all the bear watchers have played a part in such a death. As we stood on the roadside in Yellowstone admiring the bear through cameras, binoculars, and spotting scopes, we conditioned that animal to not fear humans. To not run when someone points a camera or binoculars or spotting scope or rifle at him. That conditioning is a death sentence once grizzlies have been stripped of Endangered Species Act protection.

As grim as that realization is, I don't know if I am troubled enough, ethical enough, or strong enough to avoid bear watching in Yellowstone. I would like to say that I will not be a part of habituating bears to humans. But the draw to observe one of these magnificent creatures is powerful. For now, I must live with the awareness that my bear watching can make it easier for a hunter to take a grizzly. I can't blame the death of an unprotected grizzly solely on a trophy hunter. I too am part of the problem. That's food for thought.

31

Home

———

December is near and so is the end of this year of immersion in Yellowstone's grandeur and controversy. The Grand Loop has closed for winter, and almost all park visitors have left for homes far from here. The overused park can rest for a while under a blanket of snow. Gardiner is so quiet that I can hardly believe it will be overrun again in a few months.

With the Department of the Interior's action to put mining off limits on public lands around the park, we have a break from the gold mining controversy. But that fight is far from over.

The controversial wolf hunt arrived. The quota that so many advocates fought so hard for—just two wolves in the unit bordering the park—was filled within days of the season's start. In fact, three wolves were killed before Montana Fish, Wildlife & Parks had all the information necessary to determine the quota had been reached. Sadly, all three wolves are likely from the 8-Mile pack, the wolves that led us on that fine spring meander. I'm sure that Bear Creek

Council and other conservation groups will work together next year to maintain or—better yet—reduce that quota.

As snow accumulates on the floor of the Lamar Valley, another controversy heats up. The bison have begun their long, annual migration toward Gardiner Basin, the capture facility, and the firing squad. In a couple of weeks, Leo and I will attend a tour of the capture facility and kick off another winter of worry over bison. Mary and I feel the draw of the battle against the slaughter.

This morning at breakfast Mary and I remind ourselves that the reason we moved here—left our home, family, friends, and security in Oregon—was to be near Yellowstone's grandeur. We decide that it's time to set controversy aside for a while and take a hike in the park.

Within minutes of starting down the Howard Eaton Trail, near Mammoth Hot Springs, we come upon a set of wolf tracks in the shallow snow that frosts the trail. The prints look as fresh as ours. They have not been melted by yesterday's sun nor frozen by last night's chill. We debate and eventually agree that the tracks are from a small wolf ambling in the same direction we are: toward Swan Lake Flat, four miles distant. The tracks go through territory shared by two wolf packs: the 8-Mile pack and their relations and competitors in the Prospect Peak pack.

Buoyed by the discovery of wolf tracks, we laugh and chatter and snap pictures of our hands beside them. Hoping to be lucky enough to see this—or any—wolf, we follow the tracks for about a half-mile until we reach a stand of naked aspens, their light trunks an arresting contrast to nearby dark conifers. Across from the aspens, the tracks exit the trail and enter a draw so cluttered by fallen logs that we can't hope to follow.

We stand in the middle of the trail, disappointed and silent, until Mary asks in a soft voice, "Do you think the wolf left the trail because it heard us?"

"I sure hope not. But I wouldn't doubt it with all the noise we were making," I reply, frustrated that we may have scared the animal off.

"Damn!" Mary mutters. She frowns and we look with longing at the last clear track. It tantalizes and taunts us.

But excitement dispels disappointment when we discover other tracks along the trail: coyote and fox, elk and deer, squirrel and deer mice. Each set invites us to stop, study, and speculate, as we did last winter with the tracks we found on our dawn hike to Observation Point, above Old Faithful. We have made plans to continue that new tradition of escaping the drain of winter controversies by recreating in the park's snowy interior for a few days. Yellowstone's restorative power amazes me.

We continue along the winding Howard Eaton until a gap in the trees reveals a view that slams us to a stop. Flat-topped Mt. Everts and colorful Bunsen Peak, two of the four mountains we see from our dining room window, rise close by. Near them, shadows reveal the cut of the Gardner River canyon. Farther away the snow-capped Absaroka Mountains glow in sunlight. Then there's the distant Blacktail Deer Plateau where I hiked with Leo and Mary and witnessed the cascading impact that wolves have on elk, beaver, and willows.

Farther to the east, about twenty-five miles as the raven flies, lies the Lamar Valley, our home for those three life-changing winters.

Pulling ourselves away from the viewpoint, we pick up another set of tracks, a real bonus: two wolves traveling together in the same direction we are. Mary leans toward me and whispers, "I think we should follow these tracks in silence. What do you say?"

I close my eyes and recall the joy of watching the Mollie's pack, wild and free, testing a bison herd last winter. I open my eyes, lock onto Mary's, and whisper, "Great idea. I don't want to scare these two off."

"OK. Then let's just use hand signals to communicate," she whispers back. With a forward wave of her arm, we proceed.

Over the next half-mile, we use signals we have practiced on other hikes. Without a sound, we learn from the tracks that the wolves sometimes walk beside one another, and at other times the rear wolf steps in the tracks of the lead animal. I figure that walking in the leader's tracks could be a matter of efficiency; the follower enjoys the benefit of the broken trail. But this dusting of snow does not demand efficiency. As I walk and wonder, I glance down and recognize that I am stepping in Mary's bootprints so as to avoid the wolves' tracks. Is it possible that the wolves are doing the same, to preserve the wild story their sensitive noses read? Another wonderful Yellowstone mystery.

After a while, the trail leaves the forest and enters a huge slide area. We stop and look around. The ridge above and to our right is the edge of a massive ancient thermal terrace that once was similar to the one at nearby Mammoth Hot Springs. But, as geologist Lisa Morgan explained to us last summer, Yellowstone's thermal features have changed and will continue to change. Long ago this feature dried up; the travertine aging from white to mottled gray. At some point the terrace collapsed and crashed downhill, scattering in its wake chunks—some the size of small houses, others no bigger than bowling balls. Biding their slow time, lichen grew, freckling the chunks with orange and yellow. Conifers lucked into places to sprout and grow, die and fall.

We follow the trail into the thickest part of the slide area. At the base of select chunks are dark openings. Could one of these be the mouth of a den? Is this where the two wolves, perhaps a mated pair, were headed? Biologists say that wolves often choose den sites on south-facing slopes with water nearby. I see this desire for sunshine and water in a home site as another of the many ways that wolves and humans are alike. But this slope faces east, and we don't see a source of water. So this is not an optimal site.

After deciding that only the wolves know why they left the trail, Mary and I move along, making tracks in virgin snow. When we reach the other side of the slide area and reenter conifer forest, we come upon the trail of a single wolf also heading toward Swan Lake Flat. His big tracks strut confidently down the center of the trail. We follow them to a viewpoint. His paws don't pause, but we do; we can't help ourselves. Below us is the ancient bottom of a large lake once filled by melting glaciers. Over eons the lake dried and shrank, leaving a small and shallow remnant—now called Swan Lake—and flat bottomland claimed by sage and grass. This all-you-can-eat-and-drink buffet may explain why the trail we are on is a wildlife highway. Hungry grazers take it to and from the feeding grounds; hungry predators follow.

We pull ourselves from the viewpoint and pursue the big wolf tracks that head downhill toward the lake. I take the lead, and moments later Mary breaks our code of silence with a forced whisper, "Rick, stop! Rick, stop!

I stop and look back at her as she uses her entire body to pantomime the lumbering walk of a grizzly. Her movements trigger humor and evoke caution. Then she waves me back. When I reach her, she points to the snow-covered trail and the track of a grizzly that has obviously not yet denned for the winter. The rear paw is as long as Mary's size-seven boot. And much wider. We bend down to examine another of the bear's tracks, the ball, toes, and claws of a wide front paw, my boot print in the snow beside it. I marched right by these tracks without seeing them! That's embarrassing and the reason Mary is the lead tracker in our pack.

With Mary in front, we walk on, cautious now, panning and scrutinizing. The trail, with grizzly and wolf tracks intermingling, threads through dark, thick forest. A breeze blows in our faces. Branches rustle mysteriously. As my adrenaline rises, I say, "We're behind and downwind of that bear." Mary's nods her head. "While we followed the wolf's tracks in silence," I add, "I'm not sure that's a smart move now."

She looks over her shoulder and says, volume rising with each word, "Yeah, we don't want to SURPRISE A GRIZZLY!"

As her words vanish into the thick understory, twigs snap and dried leaves crackle just to our right. We look in the direction of the sound, but see only thick vegetation. Eyes wide, we stare at each other, nod, and shout in unison the familiar chant of many previous Yellowstone hikes, "Yo, Bear! Just us! Coming through!"

We move on loudly and slowly, swiveling our heads, alert for movement. We round a bend and stop at a mess of tracks. Sorting them out, we discern that the wolf continued on but the grizzly stopped, turned around, walked about ten feet in our direction, and then vanished into the woods.

"Look at that," Mary says. "It headed in the direction from which we heard that noise. I wonder if it left because it heard us."

"I sure hope so," I reply.

We trek downhill toward Swan Lake, following the big wolf's tracks. When those tracks leave the trail, the wild wanders from our walk. As we continue on the trail, I feel relieved and disheartened.

For me, the presence of wolves and grizzlies defines wildness. Those big carnivores knock us humans from our self-proclaimed throne. So do bison, once you've encountered one at close range, as Mary and I did along Hellroaring Creek. The presence of these animals causes me to use my senses fully, to be in the moment, and to accept my humble place in nature's grand scheme.

Though each of these animals is essential to the wildlands of the Greater Yellowstone Ecosystem, I have learned in this past year that each is also under assault by humans, the only predator they must fear.

During this year, I also realized that I, like most visitors, was drawn to Yellowstone by its grandeur. And each time my limited stay ended, I left with the thought that the park would be here—and still the same—whenever I chose to return. But living in Gardiner mauled that misconception. I know now just how fragile Yellowstone is, and that it is under attack from all directions and many factions.

So many controversies became evident after we moved to Gardiner. And over the last year, I've learned that none are going away anytime soon—and none will disappear without committed and organized action. We must speak for these animals that can't speak for themselves. We must speak to the park managers, to the National Park Service, to the secretary of the interior, and to our elected officials, including the president. We must make clear how we want them to protect our public land. Like wolves in packs, we will find strength in numbers, and eventual success.

As Mary and I walk out of the woods and into the expanse of Swan Lake Flat. I look to my right and there rises snow-covered Electric Peak, the mountain we climbed a dozen years ago when we first returned to Yellowstone, long before we made our home here. And now—to our surprise and delight—from our dining room window that peak shines in the sun or plays with the clouds. Even when the peak hides, I enjoy knowing I'll see it again. Electric peak has become a touchstone; the sight of it confirms I'm home. Yellowstone is no longer a place to love and leave. And with that belonging comes a duty to fight for this wildland and its wildlife for years to come.

Rick welcomes friends, followers, and connections on these social media sites:

Blog: ricklamplugh.blogspot.com
Facebook: Rick Lamplugh
LinkedIn: Rick Lamplugh
Google+: Rick Lamplugh
Twitter: twitter.com/rick_lamplugh
Vimeo: vimeo.com/ricklamplugh

A Message to the Reader

———

Dear Reader,

I hope these stories of Yellowstone's grandeur and controversy stir you to action. You can learn more about the park, the challenges it faces, and how you can help by visiting my Rick Lamplugh Facebook page. I welcome your friend request. You can also read more in-depth pieces on my blog, ricklamplugh.blogspot.com.

There's another important step you can take.

I chose to independently publish this book because I wanted more control over the finished work. But independent publishing means I don't have the muscle of a traditional publisher to promote the book. There's just me. And you, the satisfied reader.

You can help me—and other indie authors—by taking a moment to click on Amazon.com and rate this book. Your star rating and review (no matter how brief) help other readers find books by indie authors.

Thanks for reading and helping,

Rick

About the Author

Rick Lamplugh lives near the north gate of Yellowstone National Park and writes to protect wildlife and preserve wildlands.

Rick's last book, *In the Temple of Wolves: A Winter's Immersion in Wild Yellowstone,* has been an Amazon best seller for more than three years and earned more than 265 Five-Star reviews.

Rick's stories have appeared in *Yellowstone Reports,* and the literary journals *Composite Arts Magazine, Gold Man Review, Phoebe, Soundings Review,* and *Feathered Flounder.* He won the Jim Stone Grand Prize for Non-Fiction.

Acknowledgements

It took a family to produce this book. My wife Mary—in addition to sharing all the mountains, miles, meetings, and moments—helped every step of this book's way. From the birth of the idea, to debate about endless options, to exemplary editing, to honest critique, Mary was always there. My daughter Allison Lamplugh, a skilled working journalist, read every chapter and provided valuable feedback, edits, and support. My stepson Zack Prucha and daughter-in-law Tara Hana Prucha, both talented designers, created the lovely cover that invites readers in.

During the two years of this project, my friend and fellow meanderthal Leo Leckie reviewed numerous chapters and answered unending questions both while on the trail and every other time we were together.

Two editors improved this book. First is my friend, teacher, and editor Lill Ahrens. Lill has a seemingly innate ability to know how a story should be told. Every story in this book flows better because of her touch. Second is Kathleen Marusak. Kat's skilled line editing vastly improved each chapter in this book. Lill's and Kat's enthusiasm made them a pleasure to work with on *Deep into Yellowstone*—just as it did on *In the Temple of Wolves*.

A number of chapters first saw the light of day as feature articles on *Yellowstone Reports*, a subscription-based website operated by Nathan Varley and Linda Thurston. I thank both of them for trusting me to write for their excellent publication.

I sent certain chapters to certain people to make sure that I had the facts and story straight. These helpful readers include: Karen Withrow, Fred Engel, Brenda Papera, Nathan Varley, Ilona Popper, Bill Ripple, Lisa Morgan, Linda Thurston, John Gillespie, Bob Beschta, Kira Cassidy, Dave Chambers, Steve Koehler, and Liz Purdy. Shauna Baron read the entire book, caught a number of errors, and added excellent insights. These readers made the book more accurate; any remaining mistakes are mine alone.

I sent pre-publication copies of *Deep into Yellowstone* to a number of people who know and love Yellowstone. I thank these talented folks for taking the time to read the book, send me comments, and write a blurb: Cristina Eisenberg, Beckie Elgin, Barbara J. Moritsch, Jim Halfpenny, MacNeil Lyons, Jenny Golding, John Gillespie, Julianne Baker, Lisa Baril, Nathan Varley, and Michelle Uberuaga.

Thanks, too, to all my friends on social media. Your comments, questions, and encouragement help me see the benefits of advocating and inspire me to do more.

Excerpt from

In the Temple of Wolves: A Winter's Immersion in Wild Yellowstone

The Bison's Last Ride

———

"I think it's a female yearling," Brian, the district ranger, says to the four of us standing across from him. The bison, a sad lump dusted with fresh snow, fills the space at our feet.

I nod toward Brian but can't take my eyes from the bison calf; she's beautiful, even in death. Short horns reveal her youth. Her brown eyes are still bright and inviting. I remove my glove, reach down, and feel the long hair on her side; its softness surprises me. I run my hand down her thin leg to what looks like a smooth-sided hoof. But the hoof is encircled with tiny ridges, and I, fascinated, run a fingernail over each one. George, Karen, and Mary, squatting and kneeling, are also caressing her. With no discussion, we share a reverent moment, as you would at the bedside of a just-departed loved one.

Though the four of us did not expect to begin our workday like this, when we learned at dawn that Brian needed help, we all wanted in. But first, we had to convince the ranch manager, Bonnie, to let us—all of her staff—go play ranger even though we must clean a dozen cabins, the bunkhouse, and the bathhouse by this afternoon. We pleaded and she relented. Then the four of us paraded toward Brian's cabin. I was light-footed with excitement about getting close to a bison, an animal that we admire every day as we drive buses full of participants in search of wildlife. Brian instructed us to meet him at the bison and to bring the blue sled, which is designed to carry a broken-down snowmobile but used in the park to move dead animals. George and I muscled it into the rear of a bus, the four of us clambered aboard, and I drove us to the bison.

Brian's soft voice interrupts our quiet moment with the calf. "Do you see any evidence of attack by a predator?"

We look at him and shake our heads.

He points to the blood drying around the nose and mouth and says, "That makes me think it was hit by a car."

That's a possibility since the bison was found dead on the road before dawn east of here. Her body would create a traffic hazard, and there will be lots of traffic—today is Friday, the first day of the long President's Day Weekend. At first light, she was dragged for four miles behind a snowplow to this roadside pullout. Now we are going to sled her farther from the road.

George sighs and stands. "What do you think she weighs?"

"Probably about 500 pounds, but," Brian points toward a distant stand of cottonwoods, "it'll get heavier as we pull it out there."

That's our cue to get to work. Brian grasps the front legs; Mary and George take the rear ones. They grunt and lift and roll the bison onto the sled, revealing the side that was dragged along the snow-covered road. The hide isn't damaged, a testament to its toughness. I feel a flat spot on a horn, which is made of material similar to our fingernails, and which the road filed.

Brian asks Karen, Mary, and George to tamp down a three-person-wide path across the valley floor to facilitate our pulling. As they snowshoe away, chatting about what this carcass may attract, I help Brian tie the bison to the sled. He deftly wraps a rope around the rear legs. He resembles a cowboy in a rodeo bulldogging event, so I take out my camera and frame him, the rope, and the legs. The composition intrigues me, and then I'm chagrined: I'm acting just like those pushy photographers that I poked fun at a couple weeks ago as they tried to outmaneuver one another for the money shot of those coyotes eating a dead calf. I silently scold myself and stow the camera. Brian shoots me a quizzical look.

"Is it OK for me to take pictures of this?"

He glances at the bison and then the cottonwoods and gives me an emphatic nod. "Sure. That would be great. Nobody ever gets to see the things rangers do."

Now on assignment, I bend and kneel, twist and turn, happy to be immersed in capturing these images.

When the tampers return, Brian ties one end of a long rope to the front of the sled and throws the rest forward. Lying outstretched in the snow, with short ropes extending at intervals from the main line, it looks like the harness for a dogsled team. Each of the four grabs a short line and slings it over a shoulder.

Before the team can go, Brian pulls a radio from his jacket. He listens, nods, signs off, and says, "That was the Comm Center. They just had a call from two visitors who reported hitting a bison in the dark and snow this morning." He pauses as if delivering a punch line. "They said the bison walked out in the road and hit their truck." He shakes his head, and we all laugh. "That's not how it usually happens."

After a couple of months of driving along snowy park roads, we've seen how it probably happened. Calves are always with a herd, and often that herd walks down the middle of the plowed road, the easiest path in winter. We have all watched cars barge into a herd, impatient drivers rushing to get through. In a situation like that, a spooked animal could swing its head to the side and get clipped by a careless driver. Such waste saddens me.

However death occurred, it's time for the yearling's last trip across the valley floor. I snowshoe in the deep snow alongside the pre-packed trail so I can video the procession. Breath billowing and bent forward, the four haul the sled to the top of a rise. When they head downhill, I notice that the sled is picking up speed because of gravity and the lack of anyone braking from behind. The 500-pound sled is gaining on them.

"Look out!" I yell.

Four heads snap around. Each team member jumps to the side. The sled stops right where they had been. We look at one another and then laugh about how difficult it would have been to explain to Bonnie that three of her volunteers were injured by a sleigh-riding bison while the fourth videoed the mishap.

We continue on and about three-quarters of the way to the cottonwoods, just where the trio's pre-packed trail ends, we stop in a low spot from which we can't see the road.

"Maybe we should put her here where the photographers can't see her," George says.

We settle into silence as the reality of our task hits: We are looking for the best place for others to dine on this beautiful, young animal.

Brian looks toward the road and then the cottonwoods. He purses his lips and moves his head from side to side. "Let's go a bit farther."

They drag the sled up another rise, and Brian motions us to stop. "This is a good spot." He turns and points toward the road. "Photographers will be able to shoot it from three different pullouts."

"But how will you keep them from hiking out here for close-ups?" Karen asks.

"We'll cross that bridge when we come to it." After more than twenty years as a Yellowstone ranger, Brian knows how difficult it is to contain photographers. Yet he still chooses to place the bison so they can photograph wolves and scavengers dining. I'm surprised at the influence photographers hold without knowing it.

We help Brian untie the bison, and on the count of three all of us hoist one side of the sled. The calf flops into the snow. Brian kneels, and the rough sound of his rubbing snow against the sled to remove the calf's blood eclipses any remaining levity that accompanied us here. Unsure what to do now, the four of us stand mute and stare.

At last, George asks Brian, "Can I help?"

Head down, Brian holds out his bloody work glove like a cop stopping traffic. "That's probably not a good idea."

He starts stowing ropes, and the four of us volunteers encircle the bison, mourners at a graveside. A bald eagle lands high in the nearby cottonwoods, waiting.

Brian stands, brushes snow from his knees and gloves, and states, "You know, even though this is an unnatural way for the bison to die, it will feed many other animals."

I nod in silence, thankful to be reminded of a way to see some value in this death.

Brian pulls the sled away, and the others snowshoe in silence behind, family following the hearse from the cemetery. I stay and take two final pictures. I walk to the bison's head and gaze into her brown eye, now dull. Snowflakes land on the eye and don't melt. Beneath the cottonwoods, a hungry coyote has joined the eagle. I whisper an invitation to the scavengers. I thank the bison for providing them sustenance and then turn and snowshoe toward the road without a backward glance. I figure that I know what comes next.

As it turns out, I had no idea.

Though we moved the bison just hours ago, the news of the meal-waiting-to-happen went viral among the long-weekend visitors. By noon, the three pullouts and the road connecting them look like the scene of a nasty accident. A ranger SUV, lights flashing, sits before the first pullout. Another flashes after the last one. All three pullouts are jammed with vehicles surrounded by talkative visitors. Photographers perch atop a couple of vans. People mill around in the road. At one point, a gigantic tour bus rumbles up, stops in the middle of the road, but thankfully does not disgorge its contents.

On Saturday, the photographers get into a feeding frenzy when the Lamar Canyon pack comes down from Druid Peak. Rangers stop traffic in both directions, giving ten wolves safe passage across the road. Still, with the machine gun-like clacking of motor-driven cameras and the wolves' aversion to humans, they take a long time to cross.

Once they reach the bison, one approaches the carcass, sniffs and leaps back. I assume it's repulsed by the scent from our earlier handling. I feel guilty at my selfish need to touch the calf without considering the lingering human stench. A couple of other wolves are also repelled before the pack risks opening the carcass. Meanwhile, impatient ravens croak, the eagle observes from a cottonwood, and the coyote is nowhere to be seen.

On Monday afternoon, when most of the long-weekend visitors are home or driving there, Mary and I and just three others watch the well-fed Lamar Canyon pack cross the empty road only yards from us and trot along that ridge that leads up to Druid Peak. I feel blessed to be so close, but as I watch their nervous behavior, I also feel like a nuisance.

Three weeks and three snowstorms later, Mary and I return to the pullout where we loaded the yearling onto the sled. We are curious to see what remains of the carcass. The path we made for the bison's last ride has disappeared. We don our snowshoes and head across virgin snow toward the cottonwoods. We guess our way along but can't find the remains. We squat down in the snow and wait. Just as we are starting to feel too chilled to stay, a black-and-white flash zips by. The magpie lands about twenty yards away and starts walking and pecking.

We rise and move toward it, picking up a trail of magpie tracks, each a skinny Y. We spot strands of hair and fragments of bone and center ourselves in the debris field. Mary drops to all fours and starts sweeping away snow. A few inches below the surface, she uncovers a frozen rug of bison hide. Nearby, she discovers a blood-stained bottom jaw with unworn teeth. I dig around, come up with a hoof attached to a leg bone. I take off my glove and again feel the hoof's ridges.

When I look up from the hoof, something bright and blue and about ten yards away catches my eye. With respect I put the hoof down, snowshoe the distance, and tug a ragged piece of fabric from the snow. A piece of a hat? A towel? Hard to say from what remains, but it reeks with the pungent smell of wolf. I imagine the pups using the fabric as a pull toy while the adults—satiated after dining—doze.

I snowshoe back and kneel beside Mary. She turns to me and her eyes hold both sadness and curiosity. She nods toward where she has been digging, and we begin to cover the hide and put the bones back. The bison's return to earth isn't done yet, and we don't want to interfere.

In a month or two, when the snow thaws and spring greens this valley, hundreds of species of beetles and other insects will dine on these scraps. Anything left will begin breaking down into minerals that will enrich the soil and feed the grass. Where we now kneel in snow will be a sweet spot for bison grazing near the swollen Lamar River. A mother and her calf could be drawn here by the scent of new grass. The calf, still young enough to be mistaken for a big, red dog playing near the herd, will eat its fill, enriched by the yearling we pulled here.

Mary and I stand, hold hands, and snowshoe back toward the road, closing the circle on what began as a lark and became a touching farewell and funeral service.

Now, there's a bus to drive and cabins to clean.